SP

I'm Wearing Tunics Now

Andrews McMeel Publishing
a division of Andrews McMeel Universal
1130 Walnut Street, Kansas City, Missouri 64106

www.andrewsmcmeel.com

Versions of some pieces originally published in
McSweeney's Internet Tendency and *The New Yorker*.

"We Can't Ask Your Age in This Job Interview, but Please Take
This Quiz about Rotary Phones" cowritten by Devorah Blachor.
Reprinted with permission.

"The Perfect Cocktails for Your Perimenopause Party" cowritten by
Gloria Fallon, illustrations by Marilyn Naron. Reprinted with permission.

22 23 24 25 26 MCN 10 9 8 7 6 5 4 3 2 1

ISBN: 978-1-5248-7373-8

Library of Congress Control Number: 2022941127

Editor: Allison Adler
Art Director: Tiffany Meairs
Production Editor: Brianna Westervelt
Production Manager: Chadd Keim

I'm Wearing Tunics Now

On Growing Older, Better, and a Hell of a Lot Louder

Wendi Aarons

Andrews McMeel
PUBLISHING®

To Chris

Contents

CONTENTS

Introduction

A few years ago, I was in New York City for a week-long family vacation. The day before we headed back home to Austin, Texas, my younger son, Jack, and I decided to spend the afternoon wandering around Central Park. After walking five miles that left him no worse for the wear but me with sore feet, we were caught in a sudden and heavy rainstorm that wasn't predicted by our weather apps. So, like everyone else in that part of the park, we ran over to the American Museum of Natural History for an alternate indoor activity. We waited in line outside for a good forty minutes, ignoring the throngs of wet Europeans and the aggressive umbrella sellers who'd materialized mere seconds after the first raindrop hit the pavement. Finally inside the huge, beautiful rotunda, we stood in line for another thirty minutes. Neither of us really minded, though, because we were both in a good mood, looking forward to seeing the exhibits and to our après-museum hot dogs from the Nathan's Famous cart across the street. Yes, I'm aware of what hot dogs are made of, but I don't give a shit because they are delicious.

That day, I was wearing a light wash, knee-length denim skirt I'd recently bought from Banana Republic, a t-shirt that said "LOVE IS

LOVE" in big rainbow letters, and a pair of ratty TOMS shoes—the reason I had sore feet. (C'mon, TOM.) I knew for a fact that my look was in style because I saw at least a few ten-year-old girls wearing that exact same outfit earlier in the day when I pushed in front of them at a candy store. My limp blonde hair and my messy make-up, victims of the rain and humidity, gave me a bit of a sewer rat vibe, but I was still feeling cute because I was happy, I was in New York City, and I was with my son. I was comfortable in my skin.

After many minutes and many complicated customers, some of whom had apparently never before entered a museum or talked to another human being, it was finally our turn to approach the ticket desk. Jack and I walked up to the counter and smiled at the older woman, clad just like her co-workers in a crisp blue museum blazer, sitting behind it. "Two tickets, please," I said. But before issuing them, she glanced at us and brusquely asked, "One Student and one Senior?"

Uh, what?

My startled eyes quickly swung over to the sign on the desk that listed the admission prices, and yes, at age fifteen Jack was indeed a student, but what was that other word she said? Was it "Señor"? Did she think I was a dude? I don't look like an hombre, mostly because I have trouble growing a mustache so . . . oh my god, maybe she didn't say "Señor." Maybe . . . maybe that wack job said "*Senior*"? DID SHE SAY SENIOR? How the hell could she think I'm a Senior? Unless they had a ridiculously low entry point for Seniors? My mind raced and I frantically scanned the sign again, half expecting to see "Seniors: 30+" or "Seniors: Anyone with a Single Gray Eyebrow Hair," but then in quiet, abject horror I read this instead: "Seniors: 60+." My clammy hands grasped the marble counter for support while alarm bells rang in my ears and "HOLY SHIT, THIS ASSHOLE THINKS I'M SIXTY-PLUS" caromed from one side of my brain to the other. Me? Wendi Aarons? Born in 1967? Currently dressed like an unkempt grade schooler? A Senior? Not that there's anything wrong with being a senior, of course, but I wasn't one of them. I was in my early fifties that day. A young-looking early fifties too, I thought, and not just because I was standing near *actual fucking fossils* at the time. The piece of shit Allosaurus fifteen feet to my left had at least 46 or 47 million years on me. And this ticket pushing, insensitive museum jerk thought I was SIXTY? *PLUS*? A few choice words to snap back in reply immediately popped into my head, most of them four letters long, some of them rhyming with "moddam brothertrucker," but then I stared at the pricing sign one more time. Slowly, my eyebrows raised, my head tilted to the right, and a soft "huh" escaped my lips. The senior discount would save me ten dollars. You know what you can buy with ten dollars? Two hot dogs. Maybe even crinkle fries.

A tense moment of silence descended in our corner of the packed museum lobby while I wrestled with the tremendous blow to my ego versus my deep-seated love of saving a few bucks.

Finally, my fugue state ended when my angry teenager hissed, "Mom! Just get the tickets. You're being weird!" and the long line of pissed-off people waiting behind us came into focus. "No, thank you, I am *not* a Senior," I grandly declared to the museum employee with as much condescension as a woman holding a wallet containing a Barry Manilow International Fan Club membership card was capable of. "Not even *close*! I am a REGULAR MUSEUM ADMITTANCE PERSON. I was definitely NOT alive when Kennedy was assassinated by the CIA. So, good day, MADAME." And then I concluded the horrific episode by haughtily jamming my credit card into the machine the wrong way while it angrily beeped and my son and the ticket seller rolled their eyes.

And that whole scene is middle age in a nutshell—humbling, undignified, and insulting, but also surprisingly full of perks you didn't know were in the mix. What a rush.

Right now, I'm at the crossroads of old and young. As my friend Nancy, creator of the Midlife Mixtape podcast, says, I'm in "the years between being hip and breaking one." And you know what? I kind of love it. Not all of it because there are some not great things about aging—mostly ego-related so far—but I'm delighted that I'm finally growing into the person I've always wanted to be. Smart, savvy, well-traveled. Funny, interesting, confident. I have a close circle of friends, a nice house, some professional success, and enough retirement savings that I probably won't ever have to get a job greeting people at Walmart, which is a big relief because I've never been able to pull off a vest. (I always look like a divorced dad from the Seventies.) I've also raised two happy and well-adjusted sons, three less well-adjusted cats, and a neurotic poodle, and I still deeply love the man I married in 1992 except whenever he's chewing. And, despite spending 90 percent of their time on cruises to the Panama Canal, my two elderly and loving parents are healthy and supportive. My life is good. I just wish it wasn't almost over.

Oh, I'm not dying. Not imminently, anyway. I'm not typing this from a hospital bed while a doctor half my age stands in the hallway and tells my family, "I'm sorry, but the day spa where she used her Groupon accidentally injected her forehead with a lethal amount of Botox. If her face could move, you'd see that she's in a lot of pain." No, I'm still on the right side of the dirt, as they say here in Texas. But at fifty-plus, more of my life is behind me than in front of me, and it can feel bittersweet when you realize that your roadmap will soon run out of road. Or, put in a way that doesn't sound like a corny country song, I finally got my shit together, but now I'm An Old.

Okay, fine, that could also be a country song.

It's only now that I realize that I spent too many years biting my tongue, sitting in the back, not making waves. I acted like a good girl, a good mom, a good wife, and a good employee. Many women of my generation relate to this. Most of us grew up shrinking ourselves to fit in instead of making our environments grow to fit us. We didn't have Girl Power or STEM; we had high school typing class and "Can You Pinch an Inch?" We had the Swedish Bikini Team and No Fat Chicks. The women in the movies we watched weren't the heroes, they were the pretty face and hot body that was objectified or in peril or both. Women my age are latecomers to the whole, "I'm speaking!" movement that's happening now. At least, I am. I've always had a strong, funny, opiniated voice, but it was wedged inside me, much like my hand was recently wedged inside a can of Pringles. Yes, I know what Pringles are made of, and I don't give a shit because they are delicious.

Middle age gave me my voice. And my confidence. After I turned forty, I began to walk away from what wasn't working (neighborhood mom prom) and walk toward what was (not caring about neighborhood mom prom). I now have more authentic friendships and passions than I've ever had before. With middle age came the self-assurance to finally feel comfortable in my own (pimpled *and* wrinkled, huzzah!) skin. It made me stop trying to change myself and start changing the world. It led to me being a better wife, daughter, sister, and mother because I was fulfilled and happier. And if I was able to do that, other women can too. I want us all to understand that we don't have to have our lives figured out at age thirty. Or at forty. At fifty? It's time to get your act together, baby, and let me help you figure out how.

It's a cliché to say that once a woman reaches middle age she becomes invisible. It's a cliché to say that in middle age a woman loses most of the fucks she has to give. But both of those clichés are true, and they're also related. It's freeing. I can't even explain how great it feels to walk into a bar, and for the first time in my entire life, not worry if the men in there think I'm attractive. I couldn't care less about the male gaze. And not just because I've been married for thirty years and I'm all set in the man department, thank you very much. Now I can dance badly to '80s songs with my friends and act unabashedly weird because I don't care how I look to anyone anymore. I don't feel like I need to sashay around in a bandage dress and six-inch heels, seductively sipping on a fruity drink. I'll be over here in my Old Navy leggings and Chaco orthopedic sandals chugging vodka tonics because my gastrointestinal system can no longer handle sugar after 7 p.m., and that is A-OK with me.

Saying that I don't care what other people think of me and really, truly believing it is damn liberating. Don't like my political opinion? That's fine, but I'm not going to be quiet about it anymore. I'm not going to worry that you won't like me because of my beliefs and my choice in candidates. Rather I'm going to loudly march, and block walk, and make GOTV calls like a mother. I'll even train my poodle Teddy to pee on your Ted Cruz yard sign. Yeah, that's right. It was him. Come at us, HOA—*we have no regrets.*

All of that said, I admit that I really didn't want to embrace the term "middle age" when I hit this phase of life. Who does? It seems like something to be embarrassed about or ashamed of, even though it's as neutral an age signifier as "teenager" or "twenty-something." Or "thirty-something trying to look twenty-something but looking more like a desperate forty-something because Hot Topic crop tops are always a bad idea." And, of course, the age category of "senior," which I now know should be used with great caution when addressing the general public, Blue Blazer Museum Lady. But the time has come for us all to embrace midlife. To say our real age when someone asks. To hold up forty or fifty fingers and proudly say, "I'm this many years old!" Yes, that'll take a while because that's a lot of fingers and it'll probably look like you're doing jazz hands for no apparent reason, but how about we start to think of our age as a badge of honor and not a burden?

I'm proud of my journey to get to where I am now in middle age. Yes, I just said "journey" and I'm not even on *The Bachelor*. I like to think my story is one that's inspiring. Well, sort of. I mean, I'm not Greta Thunberg. My life is privileged and I'm lucky. I won't say "blessed" because that's a fucking stupid word that should only be seen on decorative plaques in Waco, Texas, kitchens. The biggest childhood trauma I had to overcome wasn't fighting climate change skeptics, it was the Toni home stack perm my mom gave me when I was twelve that made me look like Preteen Dee Snider for three solid years. (#WereNotGonnaTakeIt) Still, even though I didn't need to triumph over adversity to gain the confidence I have now, it took deliberate yet authentic work. It took putting myself out there like I never had before. It took finding the power and strength in other women and realizing that we have the wisdom and fight to make changes both in our lives and in the world. I didn't accept the status quo, even if that was painful and humiliating at times. I had to grapple with and then find freedom in erasure, first as a mom and then as a woman over forty. And instead of blooming where I was planted, I pulled up my roots and found a new fucking garden. Yes, I'll probably cross-stitch that.

I want you to read this book and laugh but also relate and feel less alone. I want you to understand that you don't have to be pigeonholed into a boring middle-aged life or a perfect mom life or any kind of life that makes you feel unseen and unhappy. I want to inspire you to speak up and act out and not wait for your hoped-for life to find you. Think of this as *Eat, Pray, Love*, but with less yoga, pasta, and enlightenment, and more boxes of chardonnay, TV watching, and "Are you fucking kidding me?" I guess that'd probably be called *Drink, Binge, WTF,* so please let Julia Roberts know if you run into her at your local med spa.

To quote e.e. cummings for the first and probably last time in my entire life because I just had to Google e.e. cummings, "It takes courage to grow up and become who you really are." This is my coming-of-middle-age story. My creating-where-I-fit-in story. My finally-fitting-into-*myself* story. Middle-age, no-fucks-given, grown-ass womanhood is where it's at. And I can't wait to tell you all about it.

CHAPTER ONE:

I'M WEARING CHUNKY HEELS NOW

The first time I cried about being old was on my thirtieth birthday. Actually, "cried" is a nice way to put it. It was more like the unhinged sobbing you hear in a horror movie right after an ancient demon is unleashed from the bowels of hell and runs off to gobble up a pack of slutty cheerleaders. (Note: "slutty" is how we said "sex positive" in the '80s.)

My husband, Chris, and I were in the car at the time, driving down the twisty mountain road from Lake Tahoe to my parents' house in Carson City, Nevada. We'd spent the night up at Stateline, the small tourist town that straddles Nevada and California, to celebrate my "big birthday." My "big birthday," was also known as "the big three-oh," something my family had said to me repeatedly for months. "Thirty!" my mom had gasped before we headed out. "If you're thirty, that makes me ancient! Hoo boy!"

"I can't believe I have a wife who's thirty!" my two-months-younger husband gasped back. Then my mom piled on with, "Better trade the old nag in for a newer model!" and the two of them laughed and high-fived each other while I slumped off to my teenage bedroom for a pouting session. If those walls previously covered in George Michael posters could talk, they'd say, "Oh, for fuck's sake, what's the matter with Miss Sensitive *this* time?"

Despite their teasing and my mild gloominess, I still thought I was handling my looming decrepitude pretty well. I'd made an attempt to celebrate it at least. We'd flown from Los Angeles to Nevada to see our two sets of parents for the weekend. That was always a good time and a welcome break from our busy lives and jobs. Then Chris and I headed up to Tahoe for a night to party and gamble at the casinos. We are both enthusiastic yet cheap gamblers, more low-rollers than high-rollers, so "party and gamble" means we plopped ourselves in front of the nickel slots at Harrah's and drank whatever free watered-down well drinks the unlucky cocktail waitress felt like bringing us. ("Thanks, Janice. Here's a little somethings for your troublez," I'd slurred while dumping a dollar in nickels on her round serving tray.) Despite our low-roller status, the casino hotel had even upgraded us to a suite with a view of the lake, after Chris told the registration clerk that we were there to celebrate my "big birthday."

"You don't need to keep saying that," I hissed as we walked past the flashing slot machines and loud blackjack and roulette tables to our room. "You don't need to tell *everyone* I'm thirty."

"You're getting a suite, aren't you? And maybe she thought I meant your twenty-first birthday," he said, shrugging.

"Ohhh! I bet you're right," I said, mostly to convince myself. "I do look a lot closer to twenty-one than to thirty. Apologies in advance if I get carded a lot tonight considering that I'm barely legal."

"Just push the elevator button, jailbait," Chris answered, already tired of the age talk. Little did he know what was in store for him later.

My life on the precipice of thirty wasn't a bad life. Not in the least. I had my sweet husband of six years, a job at a movie studio, supportive if slightly eccentric parents and in-laws, and a cute rental house in Los Angeles that we'd lived in ever since the Northridge earthquake of 1994 semi-decimated our previous rental (including every piece of glassware we owned besides two promotional "Cheers to Roast Beef!" goblets we got for free at Arby's.) At thirty, I had nothing to complain about. Which didn't stop me, of course. So, on the afternoon of my "big birthday," as we drove away from the casino, and our car whipped past giant pine trees, the glimmering lake, and yellow signs warning us of chunky grizzly bears, I gripped onto the edge of my seat with both hands. And I lost my shit.

"I'm . . . so . . . fucking . . . oh . . . oh . . . ohhhhhhld," I wailed as Chris tried to focus on the road while also trying to reassure me that I was still reasonably attractive for my age. "I'm almost deeeehhhh . . . eaddddd. I'm such a FAILURE."

My husband is a loving guy, but he definitely has his limits with my neuroses, so at that point he just turned up the car stereo and, as he told me later, "pretended to be transporting an injured cat to the animal hospital." I can't say I blame him. I was a nuclear meltdown in a Gap Outlet skirt and chunky-heeled mid-'90s shoes. I thank the Lord there wasn't cell phone or internet technology yet, because if there was, Chris would have been tempted to send a video of me tearfully squeaking, "My . . . life . . . is . . . one-third . . . OVERRRR. . . . I'll never be a wunderkind . . . I'm . . . a . . . wizened . . . old . . . HAG" to a "White Chicks Are Crazy" Instagram account. Would've gone viral too.

All of the high drama and histrionics of that day are completely embarrassing to me now, some twenty-ish years later. Thinking I was old at thirty? Please. Of course I wasn't old. Nobody is old at thirty. It's THIRTY, for god's sake. Thirty years is only significant if you're talking about a home mortgage or an evil witch's curse that turns you into a gnome with a burning venereal disease. I'd barely even lived by that age. My body was still young and smooth and fresh. I possessed nary a dark circle or a skin tag, and my boobs were still perched in their glorious position of closer to my chin than to my belly button. I looked damn good. Which I unfortunately only realize in hindsight. Now, whenever I see pictures of myself from the early '90s, I wonder why I didn't run around town in a tiny bikini 24/7. "What's that? Swimwear isn't allowed inside this church? Well, I'm only wearing this thong to show off God's handiwork, monsignor." And man, did I look good in a belt back then. I really took having a waist for granted.

But besides reveling in my looks instead of constantly critiquing them, I also should have been reveling in all of the potential experiences and accomplishments ahead of me. I should have been making plans for the future instead of dwelling on how much of my life had already passed. So many "should haves." But I wasn't that wise yet. Is anyone? As the saying goes, "You don't know what you don't know until you know it." I couldn't foresee the many hills and valleys ahead of me. I had no idea that the choices and friendships I'd make over the next two decades would help me evolve into the person I didn't yet know I wanted to be.

I didn't know that I'd actually start to flourish, not wither, in middle-age.

So maybe that's why on my thirtieth birthday, rather than quietly counting my blessings or setting goals for the future, or journaling my deepest desires, or speaking my truth into the universe, I opted instead to huddle in the passenger seat of a Nissan Maxima with snot pouring out of my nose and holler, "I'M A GODDAMN 'GOLDEN GIRL' NOW. JUST CALL ME SOPHIA PETRILLO, ASSHOLES."

But in my defense, nothing fucks you up more than a milestone birthday.

A milestone birthday, in case you don't spend a lot of time browsing greeting cards in the grocery store while eating germ-covered cheese samples like I do, is a birthday that ends in a zero.

Everyone goes a bit crazy over them. Well, most everyone. I'm sure there are some "well-adjusted" people out there who deal with aging just fine, but I don't know any of them personally because I've never visited Make Believe Fantasyland. These milestone birthdays are kind of like New Year's Day: for twenty-four hours, you feel nauseated, hungover, and filled with regrets about your life's choices. There's also probably a bit of glitter in your pants. But it's these zero ages, these "big birthdays," that frequently spur an existential crisis and compel you to take stock of your life. (Unless you're a man, in which case "take stock of your life" likely means run out and buy something red with wheels or a shirt from UNTUCKit.)

My first two decade birthdays, ten and twenty, were, in internet language, total nothingburgers. I probably enjoyed a slumber party that included Tony's frozen pizza, Megan's frozen training bra, and *The Love Boat* and *Fantasy Island* on the first one and a few blurry beer bongs on the second. I do remember my twenty-first birthday, however, which I celebrated by drinking flaming rum cocktails with fellow film majors at the University of Oregon in Eugene. Not the best idea because my Aqua Net–doused perm was A) flammable and B) soon aflame and C) a bit crisp for the remainder of my junior year.

"You're on fire, Wendi!"

"Why sank you for notishing!"

"That wasn't a metaphor, idiot. We need a fire extinguisher!"

Back to my big three-oh meltdown and even more reasons why I couldn't deal.

Thirty was my first "big birthday" that wasn't about something fun or significant. At sixteen, you can drive; at eighteen, you can vote; at twenty-one, you can drink. But thirty? Nothing of note except a surprisingly large amount of people reminding you that you're still younger than Jesus. "The Savior was nailed to the cross at age thirty-three, so keep that in mind, Wendi," my husband's wild-eyed religious co-worker told me at their annual holiday party.

"Good to know, Tim," I answered, as I slowly backed away toward the cash bar. "I'll be sure to avoid big pieces of lumber for the next three years."

Besides being in competition with the Son of God, here's the main reason I felt like a failure at thirty: I was working in Hollywood at the time. And, by industry standards, I was gross. Nobody admits to being thirty in Los Angeles. You're better off confessing to a multi-state murder spree than confessing the year you were born. I never, ever told anyone my age. Anytime someone in LA asked me how old I was, I quickly changed the topic to unfounded gossip about Kevin Costner.

"You didn't hear it from me, but rumor has it that ol' Costy was actually born in 1899. He just has really good doctors. If you look closely at his face in *Dances with Wolves*, you can see the staples. What? No, I'm still in my twenties. Unlike *Kevin*."

At thirty, I'd been the executive assistant to the senior vice president of Warner Bros. Pictures for three years, but it was only an impressive job to the rest of the world. Not to Hollywood. In Hollywood, it meant that I wasn't even a has-been. I was a never-was. Anyone truly talented (or white or male or with the last name Eisner) was running their own production company by age thirty. Snagging their fourth Oscar or fourth husband. It was only natural that I felt washed up given that I worked in a world where lists like "The Top 25 Twenty-Five-Year-Olds" were commonplace. I was too old to even be a "30 Geniuses Under 30!" And nobody ever prints a "30 Thirty-Year-Olds Who Won't Reach Their Peak Until Fifty!" list. We'll probably never see a "Hollywood's Hottest Menopausers" headline in *Variety*.

I had lost sight of the fact that working at a movie studio in Los Angeles was in itself a small miracle, at least for me. My snobby boss grew up in Beverly Hills and was the epitome of "born on third base and thinks he hit a triple." I grew up in a small town in North Dakota, so the odds of me making it that far were pretty low. There weren't a lot of us Dakotans hanging out at the Polo Lounge in the early '90s, to say the least. Nobody from Fargo was plopped down in Spielberg's office saying, "Yah, you betcha, that E.T. fella is a great actor, dontchaknow." One day, I mentioned where I grew up to my boss, and he looked like I'd just told him that I married my first cousin while riding buffaloes and attacking the Sioux so we could steal their land. He was kind of a dick in general, but his elitist distaste of me that day and on many other days—something I experienced from both him and other Hollywood people—quashed my individuality. It reinforced my natural instinct that told me that in order to be successful and liked, I should stay quiet and hide my real self; that people would like me more if they didn't really know me or that I grew up in an unglamorous state and went to, gasp, déclassé public schools. It's that kind of thinking that compelled me to say things like, "Yes, I love sushi!" before choking a chunk of it down like a dummy and then spitting it back out instead of simply saying, "No, thank you, I prefer my fish frozen and in stick form, please." I immediately do that now, and rather loudly, but I don't want to get ahead of myself.

This idea that suppressing my personality was the only way to fit in and please others, coupled with the fact that at thirty I was still mostly the quiet reader/good girl I'd always been, meant that I never pushed back when someone at work was a jerk to me. Like a certain producer who yelled expletives at me for answering the phone wrong. ("Sorry, I'll try to remember to never say 'Good Morning' when it's 12:01 p.m. I apologize, sir, for being insensitive to the sun and its motions.") Or when I saw harassing behavior at the studio that would now be tweeted about a thousand times with the #MeToo hashtag and result in a job loss and/or prison time. I definitely felt uneasy about things I saw and heard, *believe me*, but I didn't speak up because no woman really did at the time. We were all too scared to lose our jobs. Too scared to piss off the wrong people. There weren't that many spots for women back then, so why jeopardize yours by saying, "I heard what you said about a certain actress on your phone call, and it was repulsive and misogynistic, and you are a piece of shit, and I'm reporting you to HR" to your boss?

We Gen Xers didn't grow up with the kind of widely accepted feminist messages young women grow up with today. I mean, we had some of it, but female leaders and role models weren't celebrated or highlighted all that much. Not like they are now, anyway, when you can't turn a corner without seeing a smug baby in a forty-dollar "MY QUEEN IS RBG" onesie. Yes, I'm sure I could have found some books about powerful women at the library, but I was too busy watching Tawny Kitaen roll around the hood of a car in a Whitesnake video to bother. That's why at thirty, I didn't yet realize that the reason I didn't get things like the writing fellowship at Warner Bros. had less to do with my talent and way more to do with the white bro head of the program hand-picking all his white bro golf buddies named Chad. I didn't know the game was rigged. I still remember walking into that nimrod's office to talk about the script I wrote, the script that he admitted was one of the best he read that year, and the first thing he said was, "Aren't your legs chilly in that short skirt, Wendi?" Yuck. Of course, all I did was smile and say, "Not really!" instead of cold-cocking him with one of the shiny awards he had displayed behind his desk like I hope I'd do now.

I didn't have much bravado left by my thirtieth birthday, but I actually had a ton of it when I arrived in Hollywood at age twenty-two. I was too naïve to know any better. I'd packed up my college degree and got into my beater car with three-hundred dollars in my pocket and headed to LA with no contacts, no connections, no insights, no cell phone, no husband (yet), and no real plan but to "work in the movies." My mom says, "Dad and I just stood on the curb and watched you drive away that day because nobody could tell you not to go. You were determined." Yes, but I was also barely a touch savvier than a busty country bumpkin who gets off the Greyhound with her suitcase in hand and runs off with the first pimp who tells her he's a producer. But that naïve bravery diminished the longer I stayed in LA, and I began to lose my voice.

Luckily, the grand college romance that began over a keg at a Reno fraternity party continued when Chris joined me in California after he graduated a few months later, and his presence and support saved me from getting desperate enough to take the various and creepy offers that many women in Los Angeles are offered. Most of them not that different from the bus station invitation. "I could have been a high-priced prostitute," a studio friend told me once. "If I'd played my cards right and called Heidi Fleiss back."

"That's too bad," I'd sighed. "You could have met Charlie Sheen."

Chris and I lived together in a little two-bedroom apartment in Sherman Oaks for just a year before we got married at age twenty-four in a backyard in Nevada. That seems so young to me now, but we've been married for thirty years, so I guess it worked out! We had a lot of fun in Los Angeles exploring the city together, and we loved the beach and the weather. But our almost ten years in California were also filled with riots, earthquakes, fires, the O.J. case, and the time Kevin Spacey mocked me for using a Thighmaster in the hallway at Warner Bros. (But who came out ahead in the long run, huh, Kev?) It was a lot.

So at thirty, I was over living in LA, and also over working in the film business. I was too quiet and normal to fit in with the Hollywood lifestyle and people. The compromises I saw the women executives make, and the non-stop successes I saw the white idiot men enjoy, took a toll. It all just seemed too hard. One day, I sat in my outer studio office, mouth agape, and listened to an Ivy League graduate with a law degree stand inside my boss's swank office and pitch a movie about "Chimps! And here's the best part: they talk!" and then he was basically handed a million dollars and a beachfront mansion. *What the fuckkkkk?* Movies had always been one of the great loves of my life, but I had grown to hate them during my time at the studio. Plus, if I had a nickel for every time I'd fended off advances from a powerful five-foot-three-inch man named Barry, well, I'd have a shitload of nickels—that I'd immediately blow on the cheap slot machines at Harrah's. (I should note that some of the people I met in LA were wonderful, including my friend Sandra, who is now family and who recently FedExed me THC gummies wrapped in a sock. *Which is just a joke if you're reading this and work for the FBI.*)

That first milestone birthday of my adult life was filled with a lot of unnecessary drama. But it also made me realize something: I needed to make a change. The Hollywood dream that I'd worked toward since college didn't seem to make sense anymore, and I felt too old to keep pushing. I wasn't too old, but I didn't yet have the wisdom to know that at the time. I didn't understand the ways I could make it work for me. And so, after a snot-filled car freakout and much thought, I decided to leave the film business. It felt like failure at the time, but I now know it's brave to walk away from something you've long desired if it isn't making you happy. Ask any divorcée or speed boat owner. "There are two things you don't want to see being made: laws and sausage—and I'd add movies to that list," I'd opine years later, in my North Dakota–meets–Norma Desmond drawl. "And if you buy me another drink, sweetheart, I'll tell you a little story about the deal Costner made with the devil."

Two years after that epic meltdown on my thirtieth birthday caused me to take stock of my life, Chris and I pulled up stakes and moved out of Los Angeles. I was done with the movie business, and he was done with his MBA at Pepperdine, and there was no reason for us to stay in California anymore besides the random celebrity sighting at In-N-Out Burger. We wanted to have kids, maybe, and buy a house, probably, and live in a place where people didn't wear sunglasses inside the grocery store. We debated and researched and job-hunted and decided to head to the cheap, weird city of Austin, Texas. We didn't know a single person in town, but we'd heard it was great and Chris once said, "I really like BBQ," so why not? We quit our jobs, packed up our rented condo, booked flights, and drugged our cats for the two-hour plane ride. It was time for a fresh start. Any doubts we had about moving were quashed when, on our final night in LA, we watched a low-speed police chase on the TV set in our hotel room then opened the curtains and saw the chase in real time as it passed by on the freeway next to our hotel.

"The Juice is loose!" Chris yelped, like he always did whenever there was a low-speed chase in late-'90s LA, which was every day. There couldn't have been a bigger sign from the universe that it was time for change. We landed in Austin with our two stoned cats and our two hopeful faces and drove to our new apartment, passing the beautiful Lady Bird Lake, then called Town Lake, and the gleaming pink granite Texas State Capitol building. I felt like that long-lost bravado I had when I was twenty-two was finally coming back. I didn't yet know how much I was about to grow and change, or that what I'd do over the next twenty years would take me to the steps of that very capitol. Mostly, I didn't realize that at age thirty-two, I'd made it through Adult Identity Crisis No. 1 only to head straight into Adult Identity Crisis No. 2. But that was okay.

I was still one year younger than Jesus.

CHAPTER TWO:

I'M WEARING MATERNITY PANTS NOW

Nobody told me how lonely and boring new motherhood would be. Or maybe they did but I wasn't listening because is there anything lonelier and more boring than talking about new motherhood? God, no. That's why I barely survived it.

My plan was never to be a stay-at-home mom. Or a SAHM, which is how people who hate hyphens spell it. But that is indeed what I was just eighteen months after leaving somewhat glamorous Los Angeles for a brand-new life in an Austin, Texas, cul-de-sac. "Why do they call us 'stay-at-home moms,' anyway? It's not like we're chained to the oven all day, right?" I once said to a Twinset Mom while we watched our squishy sons roll around on the mat at Gymboree class. They were happily smacking each other with their sticky baby paws, so I thought we moms would get along too. I was wrong—much like I'd be the next one million times I'd try to make a mom friend.

"You shouldn't make sick jokes about women being held in captivity," was her icy response as she picked up her Winnie the Pooh diaper bag in one arm and her squishy son in the other. "Let's go over here by the nice bubble lady, Ethan."

My son Sam wasn't talking yet, but when I looked down at him on the green and purple mat, I'm pretty sure the expression on his face said, "Dial it down, weirdo. I'd like to be invited to at least a few birthday parties this year." In my defense, *What to Expect When You're Expecting* doesn't have a chapter on how to avoid being profiled as Serial Killer Mom at baby gym class and it totally should.

How to Not Become Known as Serial Killer Mom at Baby Gym Class

Do: Sit and socialize with the other moms
Don't: Sit outside the building and take photos of the other moms with a telephoto lens

Do: Catch bubbles on your hand
Don't: Carve a pentagram on your hand

Do: Eat string cheese and crackers at snack time
Don't: Loudly wish the baby gym served fava beans and a nice chianti

Do: Sing along to "Wheels on the Bus"
Don't: Ask the baby gym to blast Judas Priest

Do: Compliment the other moms on their complexion
Don't: Ask how they get their skinsuit so soft

The first few years of the 2000s (I still don't know what to call that decade—oughts? aughts? oots?) were a whirlwind. Chris and I moved to Austin, bought our first house, got jobs, lost jobs, lost our insurance that came with the jobs, and then I gave birth to Sam and, two years later, to his brother Jack. Any one of those life changes should have sent me straight into the caring arms of an Eileen Fisher–wearing therapist named Jody, but experiencing all of them in just three years meant my facial expression from the ages of thirty-four to thirty-seven was, "The fuck just happened?" I always looked like I was either walking away from an explosion or from Jeff Spicoli's pot-smoke-filled conversion van in *Fast Times at Ridgemont High*. Hey, bud, let's party! Right after I change this diaper and figure out a way to pay my eleven-thousand-dollar hospital bill.

Chris and I didn't regret the move to Austin for a second, but it took us a while to get our bearings. Back then, Texas was more like another country than another state. It's the size of another country too. As Texans are happy to tell you, "We're bigger than France!" Lone stars and Texas flags cover everything. Longhorn cattle graze in fields next to the airport. And Texans are overwhelmingly friendly, a huge difference from LA where someone once walked up to the table we were sitting at in a restaurant and took two chairs away without even acknowledging our presence. In Texas, that wouldn't happen without the stranger first introducing themselves, telling us why they needed the chairs in explicit detail, then shaking our hands good-bye after inviting us to their bible church. We also heard words and pronunciations in Texas we'd only before heard on TV. After the nice woman who helped us open a bank account drawled, "Y'all wait right here because I'm a fixin' to go make a copy on the Zee-Rox," we looked at each other with big eyes as soon as her back was turned.

"Does this bank have a cee-ment pond too?" we giggled. "Who's guarding the vault? Jethro Bodine? Maybe we can open a Hee Haw IRA!"

Ah, the perverse joy when a honky from North Dakota finds someone else's accent humorous.

Another big change for me when we moved to Austin: I switched careers. Once we'd decided to leave LA, I spent countless nights and weekends working on a copywriting portfolio because, true to my late-bloomer nature, I realized at the advanced age of thirty-two that advertising might be a good fit for my latent writing and creative skills. My epiphany was less, "I feel I have a calling to communicate with the masses" and more "There's got to be a way I can monetize my inherent ability to make up jingles about tacos." I took to copywriting like a duck to water. I *loved* it. I foresaw tons of awards and fancy titles in my future. Probably a Superbowl ad or two. I'd be just like Michael on *Thirtysomething* (never Elliot). Therefore, I was thrilled when a cool downtown Austin ad agency immediately hired me to write radio and print ads for a Lubbock, Texas, grocery store chain. I was in my thirties and being paid to be creative for the first time in my life.

"In the sixth grade, I made a poster that said, 'Hey You in Those Wedgies, Buy Some Veggies' for the local A&P store and they hung it up over the cheese case," I proudly told my skittish new boss, who wasn't quite sure what to do with my all-ads all-the-time enthusiasm. "So I was pretty much born for this."

"Stop trying to rhyme 'brisket' with 'fantastic' and we're good," he answered with a tight smile. "We're just selling meat here."

My wonderful new Austin career came with the added bonus of wonderful new acquaintances, some of whom I'd still be in touch with decades later. Thank god for that because my ad agency co-workers were truly the only people I knew in town besides Chris. They were all welcoming and fun and showed me the Texan friendliness the state is famous for. They took me to Austin's live music shows and to the town's myriad Tex-Mex and BBQ restaurants, and after a few months, I finally began to relax. "Your shoulders start to move away from your ears the longer you're in Austin," I've heard people say, and it's true. The intensity and uncertainty of LA was beginning to melt, just like the bowls of queso I was eating non-stop. (Note: In Austin, a meal of tortilla chips and gloppy cheese is both normal and applauded. A refreshing change from body-conscious Los Angeles where I was once told by a woman in a Santa Monica boutique that they "don't carry large sizes" like mine. I was a size six.) I had a new hometown, career, and friends, and a beautiful house that we actually owned instead of rented. And then, after months of trying, we were finally pregnant. Well, I was pregnant. Let's not do that whole "we" thing when only one of us had another human growing inside of her and a raging case of puffy cankles. But both of us were thrilled, scared, and feeling at least a hundred other emotions about expecting our first child. It was all happening. All of the adulting was happening. One warm spring night, I stepped outside our house, waved to a neighbor, and for the first time in a long time, felt completely awash in peace. I was now a grown-up. I no longer felt like the failure I thought I was when I had my epic birthday meltdown that still makes Chris roll his eyes and mutter, "God, that was a close one" under his breath. After years of not feeling settled or accomplished, everything in life was finally headed in the right direction for old Wendi.

And then I was laid off when I was five months pregnant.

There aren't a lot of job options when you have a stomach big enough to screen a 70mm movie on. Still, I tried my best because I couldn't fathom not working. I waddled into one of the only meetings I was able to get, and the executive said, "I don't know nothing 'bout birthin' no babies! Haha! Also, we, um, filled the position two minutes ago." I cheekily told another place that I was "interviewing for two" but that didn't work. The closest I got to being hired by anyone was when a United States Marine Corps recruiter at an unemployment job fair looked at my pregnant belly and shrugged, "Eh, we can work with that." Encouraging, yes, but I knew I'd fail his recruitment test as soon as he saw that I can only do two pushups before I pass out and need an EMT to bring the paddles. So with no job and no prospects, and the reality that any job I could get with my not-exactly-in-demand jingle-writing and movie-business skills would barely pay for childcare, I had no choice but to chain myself to the oven and become a stay-at-home mom. Yay.

Before I continue, let me say this explicitly: *I know I was lucky and privileged to stay home.* Lots of women make that choice and thrive; others wish they could but are forced to work. And many others feel they have no option but to stay home, and due to disposition or circumstance or a deep-seated hatred of The Children's Television Workshop don't 100 percent love it. (Not me, I stan Elmo.)

Back to my personal motherhood misery.

It's a strange thing to feel lonely as a new mom because you're with your kids all day. You're literally *never* alone. I know it's a hack cliché, but I didn't pee without someone watching me for at least five years straight. (That sounds creepier than I meant it to sound.) (Also, I'm now thinking a re-watch of *Showgirls* is in order.) I was with my sons Sam and Jack 24/7, making googly faces and singing songs and worrying my brain was turning to mush. My ad agency friends were busy working, my friends in LA were in LA, my parents and sisters were in Nevada, and Chris was either at his office or on business trips. He was jealous of my time at home, and I was jealous of his time *not* at home, and we felt a strange new tension in our marriage of ten years. It's an odd thing to suddenly have little bundles of love come between you and your big bundle of love. I'd hear myself yelling things at Chris like, "Well, if you'd been home to change his last ten diapers, then you'd know what I'm talking about!" and wonder what the hell had happened to me. I used to be fun. He used to be fun. Now we were fighting over whose turn it was to wipe baby food off the cat.

Some of those long new mom days were filled by children's activities or meeting up with the few friends I had in my baby playgroup. But most of the time the only social interaction I had was with random moms at the park who'd say things like, "Being a mom is the hardest job in the world!" and then I'd momentarily forget to not be myself and try to be funny, and say, "No, I think it's probably neurosurgeon or Chuck Norris's toupee wrangler, haha" and then the park mom would find some excuse to move away to another bench. Lather, rinse, repeat like a fucking battery-operated Fisher-Price toy.

Many days I'd gaze out the window at my neighbor's Bush/ Cheney sign and my other neighbor's minivan covered in Jesus decals and my other neighbor power washing her house for the tenth time in a season because her "special vitamins" gave her "so much energy!"— and good news, she was also "selling them!"—and wonder if I'd survive my cul-de-sac. Other days I'd wish I'd taken the United States Marine Corps up on their offer to enlist. At least then I'd get to travel and chant in a group setting.

I'd just started to figure out who I was with my new city and my new career, and now I'd gained two babies but completely lost myself. That's a common complaint of new moms, but I think it's felt even more so by women who were previously career-focused. I never planned to not work. I never even really planned to have kids until I turned thirty-three and my biological clock started banging pots and pans and screaming, "YOUR UTERUS WANTS SOME

FUCKING ACTION!! HURRRYYYYY!" Ever since high school my identity had been wrapped up in what I did for a living or what I wanted to do for a living, be it talent agency assistant, movie studio peon, network media buyer, or copywriter. I worked at Port of Subs as the Oil and Vinegar Midshipman for three days one summer and took it so seriously that I made my sisters salute me when they came in for lunch. (Okay, fine, that was just because I thought it was hilarious.) I loved being a mother, but I hated that my only identity now was "mother."

"You know, my life is so pathetic that if I ever end up on the news, they'll say, 'Wendi Aarons, a mother of two from Austin' and not something more impressive like 'Wendi Aarons, an award-winning filmmaker from Austin' or 'Wendi Aarons, controversial former girlfriend of George Clooney,'" I once grumbled to Chris.

"Maybe you should be more concerned about why you'd be on the news in the first place," he answered. "And leave your George Clooney fantasy life out of this. He's done nothing wrong."

But just like *Orange Is the New Black* showed us, even prisoners need gal pals, so I tried my best to meet my local mom versions of Crazy Eyes and Big Red. Key word: tried. I felt like Goldilocks tromping around town in an unlatched nursing bra and stained Keds. The moms group I attended where the white women sang Guatemalan lullabies and the babies had names that are nouns—"Put that cracker down, Equity"—and a woman with blonde cornrows gave a presentation on making your own baby wipes with cloth napkins and a bottle of olive oil? Too crunchy. Plus, why would you want your baby's booty to smell like Olive Garden breadsticks?

The neighborhood mom group filled with women named Mary Beth and their babies who were named after banks and men's bespoke clothing stores—"Put that cracker down, Brooks"—wasn't too crunchy; it was too stick-up-the-assy. The women were all nice to me, mostly because I was also white and blonde and lived in a nice house and could bust out a sorority song if threatened, but that's where the similarities ended. Racism and entitlement weren't as openly blatant in the early 2000s as they are now when the quiet woman who sold you a candle at the preschool craft fair later posts "THE WHITE RACE IS UNDER SEEGE!!!!" on Facebook, but it was still enough to make me uneasy. Like when a neighbor proudly said that she made her Latina housecleaners park on another street because she didn't want to see their low-rent car from her bay window. Yikes. Or when another mentioned the designer handbag allowance her husband gave her. A grown-ass woman *with a designer handbag allowance.* That told me A) she had no income of her own, B) she was majorly undervaluing her contributions to the family, and C) there probably wasn't going to be a twenty-fifth anniversary party in her future. Maybe I was just jealous because I knew if I asked Chris for a purse allowance, he'd be laughing too hard to throw my seven-dollar Merona insulated lunch sack at my face.

There was one sweet neighborhood mom who was always nice to me, and I appreciated that. Unfortunately, she usually wore a Che Guevara–style hat inexplicably bedazzled with a giant cross, like she was some kind of Christian rock video back-up dancer, and I always had to stop myself from asking where the revolucionarios were hiding. Costco? Babies"R"Us? The third row of her Honda Odyssey? One day at the park, she was completely distraught because her husband had lost his job, and she bravely told the group of us moms sitting on a bench, "Y'all, I know that the best thing we can do about him getting another job is to pray about it. Jesus won't let us down."

"Probably not," I remember saying as gently as I could, while keeping one eye on my kid dangling from one arm on the jungle gym.

"But it still might be a good idea to freshen up your husband's resumé. You know, in case Jesus isn't plugged into which Austin accounting firms are hiring right now."

I joke about it, but I don't have any issues with people of faith. I grew up in the Lutheran church and was both baptized and confirmed. The double whammy. But it was strange to suddenly be surrounded— and silently and not-so-silently judged—by so many Christians in Texas. The neighborhood moms regularly asked me what church we attended. That was their second question after asking me how old my kids were. In LA, the second question would be, "Who's your agent?" Maybe those questions aren't that different now that I think about it. But attending church is one thing and handing out "You're going to hell if you don't pray" comic books to trick-or-treaters, like one big-eyed mom on our street did, is another. (And boy, was that a fun Halloween conversation to have with my little traumatized vampire. "Eat your Kit Kat, Sam. I promise I'll keep Satan away.")

Whenever I was asked the church question in Texas, which was often, I briefly thought about telling the asker the truth, which was "The last church I went to was in LA and that turned out to be a cult that was later featured on MTV! Glad I didn't take up their offer to be baptized in that industrial water tank!" or simply, "We're not religious." The latter is what I easily say now. But back then I wasn't honest because I didn't want to isolate the only friends I kind of had and sort of wanted, so I'd just mumble something like, "Oh, we haven't decided on a church yet," and then hope I wouldn't say the Lord's name in vain until I got inside my car. "Jesus Chri—I mean, cheese and crackers! That's a huge bug!"

None of the moms I met back then was my Goldilocks "just right" by a long shot. Not hardly. But they were available, and I was lonely, and I wanted my sons to have friends too. That was the main reason.

From the time they're born, it gets hammered into your head that kids need to be socialized lest they start kindergarten feral and attack the teacher during circle time. And kids always have fun together because they're kids. They're happily running around the park, not trapped on a couch listening to some preschool mom brag about the "push present" her husband bought at the James Avery religious jewelry store.

At the social events we attended back then—meaning children's birthday parties— I sometimes hung out with the dads drinking beer in the backyard. They were basically a bunch of cargo-shorts-wearing dorks, but at least they weren't endlessly talking about breastfeeding and sleep schedules like the moms in the kitchen. Have you ever had to plaster a smile on your face while some woman with a Kate Gosselin haircut details her kid's past twenty-four hours of sleep? Sweet Jesus, the CIA should put that move in their secret manual of torture techniques. "At 2 a.m., he was on his right side. And then at 3 a.m., he turned to his left side!" The dads weren't much more exciting, but they tolerated me until the point when movies were brought up and they realized I knew way more than they did and had no compunction about correcting them. ("No, Jim, Scorsese's first feature film was *Who's That Knocking at My Door*, not *Mean Streets*. Please pass the queso.") They'd then switch the topic to football or carburetors or something else that made their testosterone sing and me leave.

I told my Los Angeles friend Sandra, who I'd worked with at Warner Bros., about how I was so desperate that I hung out with the dads and said in a pathetic tone, "I hope nobody thinks I'm a husband-stealer."

"I wouldn't worry about that," she laughed, no doubt thinking of the picture I'd sent of me and the boys and my sensible new mom haircut and pleated khaki mom pants I'd recently adopted. "Not unless their type is demented Sunday School teacher."

There were a lot of moments during my unsure and desperate new motherhood that I'd like to forget, but one of them I never will. I'd been up all night with baby Jack, and then toddler Sam needed me at 5 a.m. for something urgent like string cheese. Chris was out of town, and I had no friends or family to help out for even an hour, so I was exhausted. After a long, hard SAHM day, I saw my neighbor Kelly across the street at the grade school bus stop, and, feeling like I needed some adult interaction to maintain sanity, I plastered a happy look on my face and walked over with the boys. Kelly nicely greeted me, then she introduced me to the three other neighborhood moms standing with her. One by one, they each gave me a fake smile, then immediately turned their backs and started talking to each other like I didn't exist. I stood there awkwardly with my kids until the bus showed up, on the verge of tears. Kelly later called me and said, "Sorry about that earlier. They're great girls, but they said they already have enough friends." What the fuck? Who says they have enough friends? Even if they do? *Who acts like that?*

To this day, I wish I'd written down all of the profane names I called those women in my head. I'm very creative when I'm livid, and a lot of words rhyme with Bus Stop Bitches. But the moment hurt enough that I'm still stewing about it over a decade later.

In just a few years, I'd gone from literally rubbing shoulders with movie stars to middle-school-style snubs by women whose favorite actor was the cucumber in *Veggie Tales*. If I was too normal in LA, in Austin I felt too weird. Too quiet and also not quiet enough. I felt like all of the other moms were part of a club that I'd never really thought I'd want to join. And yet, I dearly wanted to join it. I wanted to fit in so badly that I kept my mouth shut whenever they said things that I didn't agree with. The bravery and confidence and swagger that I'm so proud to have now hadn't developed yet and wouldn't for a while.

Oh, would that I could go back and deliver a stinging Julia Sugarbaker speech, rather than just walk away, to the woman who said she didn't dress her son in pink because she didn't want him to be gay. "Just so you know, and your children will someday know, and their children will then know, that's the night the lights went out in GEORGIA, *you homophobic small-minded fuckfaced bitch that doesn't deserve to even live on the same planet as a gay person. GOOD DAY, MA'AM."*

New motherhood kicked my ass in every and all ways. I know I was a really, really good mother to my boys when they were small. Like, surprisingly good. My mom was even kind of shocked by how good, and she's told me that many times. ("We were all a little nervous at the start!") And Chris and I had a lot of fun with them, which I only realize in retrospect when I look at old photos and get weepy and start off-key singing "Cat's in the Cradle." But what I remember the most about those years is how I just wanted to meet other women like me. Not like me in the blonde, whitey sense, but in the ambitious, funny, and caring about larger things in the world sense. I knew those women were out there; I just didn't know where or how to find them. I was in my thirties, in a new city, with no job and no career identity, and two very cute toddlers attached to me at all times. There isn't a Tinder for Moms ("swipe right if you feed your kids organic!"), and I couldn't exactly cruise through all of Austin's city parks until I met someone else who possessed both children and a love of Barry Manilow. All I wanted was to find where I fit in.

How great would it be to have a way to match with the moms you'll like right away? Rather than showing up to a playdate and being horrified to learn that they have an entire room decorated in a clown motif? Or that they call their husband "King"? (True stories, both of them.) Maybe my mom life would have been better if there'd been an online Mom Friend Finder quiz, like:

1. What is the best way to feed your baby?
a) Bottles
b) Breasts
c) Bottles of Diet Dr Pepper balanced on breasts

2. You should brag about your child's accomplishments:
a) 24/7
b) Only when there's a lull in the conversation
c) When she gets into Harvard and not a moment sooner

3. My main topics of conversation are:
a) My child's sleep schedule
b) My child's eating schedule
c) Who's hotter: '80s Brad Pitt or '90s Brad Pitt?
   (Defend your thesis.)

4. I think it's really cool when white people name their child after Black jazz artists like Thelonious Monk.
a) True
b) False
c) Are you fucking kidding me?

5. I finally lost my baby weight when my child turned:
a) Three months
b) Three years
c) Thirty-three and a half

A bit of salvation finally came when the boys were a little older and I discovered something that changed my life: church preschool. Or, as it was called in Texas back then, Mother's Day Out. Yep, you read that right: *Mother's Day Out.* Mother's Day Out makes it sound like we were all desperate housewives dumping off our kids and then running off to the store in our pedal pushers to buy cake ingredients. (That is actually kind of accurate, now that I see it typed out.) But this Mom Rumspringa gave me three or four hours a couple times a week to just be alone. I didn't do much besides poke around bookstores or sit in a coffee shop and stare at people in a creepy, tired way. For the first time in years, I was able to be myself for at least a little while, and I started to get my mojo back. Do people still say "mojo"? Or is that a '90s thing? It doesn't matter because the point is that those free hours led to me finally coming out of my mom fog.

Five years after we became parents, Sam "graduated" from his Mother's Day Out Pre-K. He stood in the front of the church with his class that day, with his slicked down hair and little shirt and tie and waved to Chris and me in the pews with the other parents. The two of us held hands, proud that our cute, smart boy had done so well, but also proud of ourselves for surviving the challenging first years of parenthood. We knew the ceremony was kind of silly, but it also was a milestone for us. We'd all grown and matured, sometimes painfully. My feelings of being an outsider and not having any other identity than "mom" were still there, but I eagerly said "hi" to the put-together other moms and they warmly greeted me back. In my head, I'd fooled them into thinking I was just like them. I'd once again faked it 'til I sort of made it.

The ceremony began that day, and as the room quieted, I relaxed a bit and thought, "I blended in and despite my outsider-ness, I made it work. Everyone here thinks we're nice and normal and that I know how to put together a well-balanced meal that contains a vegetable." Then, against the backdrop of beautiful church banners and stained-glass windows and a giant cross, the smiling, kind minister walked past the adorable graduates and handed each child a bible. My little golden boy, the one I'd thrown all of my lost career and friendship efforts into, the one that had changed the trajectory of my life, glanced down at the book in his hand with a confused expression. He then looked into the crowd, waved at me and Chris, and yelled at the top of his lungs, "Look! He gave me a beeblay! Wow! So many words!"

Almost fitting into mom world was great while it lasted.

CHAPTER THREE:

I'M WEARING TWINSET SWEATERS NOW

OPEN on a grade school gym. It's bustling with noisy kids and shushing teachers, all sitting in rows, all waiting for the morning assembly to begin. Lining the walls are yawning parents holding travel cups of coffee. They're chatting with each other, ready to put their hands over their hearts and join in the Pledge of Allegiance and then the Pledge to Texas (yes, that's a thing). In the corner, standing by herself and dressed like she just escaped a humanitarian crisis, is WENDI, who likes to tell people that she's lost her baby weight but that ass ain't fooling anyone. She smiles sleepily and waves to her son Sam when he catches her bleary eye, but her real focus is on the other moms. She scans the gossiping groups of them with a knowing squint. She moved a few times as a kid and considers herself fairly adept at figuring out the social layout of any new environment. And so far, the cliques in this joint are textbook.

- Popular Moms: Blonde—some by nature, most by salon— fresh manicures, Lululemon leggings, toned booties, wear pink on Wednesdays. Husbands are named Trey.

- Wine Moms: Wear sunglasses indoors, carry coffee cups that say, "This may or may not be pinot," perma-tan because they spend most of their time on a boat. Husbands are named The Chadster.

- Jock Moms: Visors, tennis skirts, workout clothes that they actually sweat in. Will definitely hit you up to join them in a 5K at some point.

- Overachieving Volunteer Moms: Personalized clipboards, sensible bangs, khakis, dented minivans, spend more time at school than the teachers. Kid will get early admission to the Ivies.

- Goth Moms: (We can skip this one because the closest we came to this at our school was a woman with a Live, Love, Laugh tramp stamp.)

And of course, over in an empty hallway scandalously flirting with an older married dad, Sexy Mom, who'll be knocked-up and divorced by spring break.

Cut back to Wendi. She adjusts her pleated cropped pants *that everyone wore back then, so save the fashion judgment,* and sighs. She knows that she needs to find her mom group if she's going to survive this school for the next six years. She also knows she'll have to hide most of her liberal, agnostic, big-fan-of-using-f-word-as-an-adjective personality to fit in. But she's done it before. She fucking knows how to fucking blend in. At least she hopes she does.

Cue: "Wouldn't It Be Good" by Nik Kershaw as Wendi slowly clomps her Clarks sandals over to a nonthreatening mom wearing a baseball cap bedazzled with a cross and the word FAITH. The woman gives Wendi a quick smile, perhaps expecting a hat compliment that she won't be getting. Wendi casually leans against the wall and flicks an imaginary cigarette.

WENDI

Hi. I'm new here. Got any kids my kids' age?

END SCENE.

I hated high school the first time around. I hated it even more when I went back as a forty-year-old. When Sam started kindergarten, then two years later, when Jack did, I missed them desperately each morning after they headed out the door wearing backpacks big enough to tip them over. I mostly missed them in a Stockholm Syndrome kind of way, of course, because I also felt loose and liberated, like I'd just wrestled off a giant pair of sweaty Spanx that I'd been trapped in for years. I now had six free hours a day to once again be the creative, ambitious person I was before I had babies. Six hours! I was giddy. My mind spun with the possibilities. Should I get a job? Despite not having marketable skills in the current economy? Freelance? Write a screenplay? Take part-time work that'd barely cover the cost of after-school childcare? Or maybe invent something that would make me rich? Like edible potholders? ("They bake while you use them!")

Well, no. Most of that didn't happen or wouldn't for at least a few more years. I mostly cleaned the playroom and disinfected toilets. But I didn't have as much free time as expected, either. I naively thought having kids in school would be like the olden days when Ma and Pa

Ingalls pushed Half Pint out the door for her five-mile trek to the learnin' lean-to, then they happily spent the day churning butter and chopping wood, with maybe a little afternoon prairie delight on the straw mattress. It was not like that. At all. Because while moms of young kids can be a bit extra, grade school moms? They're *extra* extra. Picture Reese Witherspoon in *Election*, but instead of "Tracy Flick for President," the sign on her card table says, "Wish a motherfucker *would* tell me she can't volunteer for Field Day." It's intense.

During the K–5 years, parents are needed/wanted/expected to be present for class parties and field trips and test monitoring and special PE weeks and carnivals and book fairs and science nights and good-god-we're-going-to-get-the-most-out-of-these-years-with-our-adorable-grade-school-kids-if-it-kills-us festivals. It's nonstop. So. Many. Sign-up. Sheets. Nobody starts off as a grade school parent thinking they'll one day wrestle over a pen with a surprisingly strong Mormon woman named Ellen who's hell bent on being next year's third grade room mom, but guess what, dipshits? (I let her win, for my own survival.)

The volunteer strategy I'd perfected in pre-K—sign up to bring napkins to the class party, then fill my trunk with napkins because I will forget them on the day I need to bring napkins because I never know what the date is unless it's Christmas or my birthday—was now shameful. No mom besides me would dare to lower themselves to bring *paper goods*. They wouldn't dream of contributing something that came *in a package*. Instead, they plopped down perfectly symmetrical apple slices, frosted theme cookies, chocolate fountains, and other fancy things you'd see at a Russian mafia boss's daughter's wedding right before a rival gang shows up to end the night in a bloodbath. The second-grade holiday party of 2008 was just one jazz quartet and swan ice sculpture away from being a norovirus-infected cruise ship banquet.

"I can't compete with the other moms in Sam's class," I whined to Chris one night after collapsing on the couch, exhausted and sticky from an afternoon spent at two holiday parties. "Some of the moms actually brought homemade fruit skewers today."

"You know fruit skewers are just chunks of pineapple stabbed with a stick," he answered carefully. "I think even you could probably figure that one out, Martha Stewart."

"Thanks for your confidence," I sighed. "But you know my real strength is Kimberly-Clark products."

Many Gen-X moms were fixated on being Great Moms in the early 2000s. I know I was. We eagerly read all of the parenting books and magazines for guidance on how to best raise our kids. We followed mommy blogs, which is what "parenting influencers" were called in the dark ages, and we would have listened to podcasts if they'd been invented yet. Like me, most women in my neighborhood didn't work outside the home because one income was still doable in Austin back then. (Now, you're lucky to buy a literal shack for under a half a million dollars here.) Because we didn't have real fears like a pandemic or government coups, it was also the glory days of The Mom Wars, with everyone fighting a meaningless battle to make their version of motherhood win. Mom blog comment sections were filled with nasty arguments over breast vs. bottle, spanking vs. not spanking, working moms vs. SAHMs, and will your child grow up to be a psychopath if they don't eat organic? (They will not.) It seems quaint now, when there are daily Facebook battles over whether or not Tom Hanks and Hillary Clinton run a pedophile ring out of a pizza parlor and drink newborn baby blood. (They do not.) But that intensity, plus the burgeoning helicopter parent movement that was taking off, made me suspect even then that most moms weren't volunteering in order to make their kids happy. They were putting in hours to keep up with the Joanses.

Before too long, so was I.

Much like nature abhors a vacuum, the PTO abhors a woman trying to figure out her pathetic life when she could instead be ineptly cutting out construction paper decorations for the class St. Patrick's Day party. ("Thanks, Mrs. Aarons, for the . . . one-leaf clovers.") I really didn't want to volunteer, mostly because large groups of children terrify me. Want to hear someone yell that your butt is too big? Walk past any playground. But it felt selfish and wrong to even think about focusing on my own ambition. It felt indulgent to put my needs first. None of the other women at school were trying to be #BossBabes, besides the random MLM pushers who were to be avoided at all costs lest you end up with a seventy-five-dollar potato peeler. So how could I not help out on Foot Feelie Day when I didn't *really* have much else to do? Or not put on a fuzzy sweater and get excited when my adorable little boys asked if I'd be at their Valentine's Day parties? Chris was at his office and unable to go to most of their activities during the day, so, like most women, I was the default parent. The Mom Guilt was too much if I voluntarily missed something.

Another main reason for volunteering was that, just like in Pre-K, I dearly wanted my kids to continue to fit in and have friends. And the key to that was fitting in and having friends myself. I didn't want anyone to say, "Oh, you're not allowed over at the Aarons house because they're not our kind of people." True, I wasn't exactly young Ozzy Osbourne slinking through the hallways with a sacrificial bat head on a stake, ready to lead the kindergarten class into Satanism or at least into the metal rock scene, but I was still a little "edgy" for our vanilla school. At least I was in my own mind. I pictured myself as misanthrope chain-smoker Janeane Garofalo in *Romy and Michelle's High School Reunion* dressed all in black and battling the perfect popular pastel girls. So I decided to help out as much as I could at school and show everyone that I was a "good parent." That I was just like one of them, nice, normal, and trustworthy. My dumb strategy worked, just like I knew it would, and before long the social invitations started to come my way. I accepted each and every one of them.

It was time for Mom Prom.

OPEN on a suburban living room. The beige walls are plastered in decorative religious crosses. Metal, wood, ceramic, yarn. Like hundreds of crosses. Like Jesus himself would say, "Whoa, now that's a bit much, girlfriend. I *get* it. You *like* me." Groups of white women sit at three tables, all excited to be playing a dice game famous in the suburbs. WENDI sits quietly at the dining room table sporting her Mom Haircut and Mom Twinset.

WENDI

Excuse me, but it's my first time playing this.
Is there wine? I thought this game was called
"Drunko." Or do we just play dice sober
and talk about Ethan's rash all night?

HOSTESS

It's called Bunco in my house! Wine is
for communion. Love your sweater, gurl!

OPEN on another suburban living room. No crosses on the wall in here, but plenty of HomeGoods wall art about LOVE and FAMILY and KINDNESS. There's a sign telling you you're in the KITCHEN and another one telling you that's where you EAT. Above the washing machine is a LAUNDRY sign. Wendi wonders if the people who live here are all MORONS that don't know what ROOM they're in. She sits uneasily on a Pottery Barn couch between two other moms while an intense blonde woman in the middle of the room gives an animated sales pitch for Pampered Chef products.

> WENDI
> (whispers to the mom on her left)
> Hey, I'm a little freaked out because I think I just saw a Confederate flag when I went to the bathroom.

> MOM ON LEFT
> Probably! Bridgette's ancestors fought in the Alamo! She's really proud of her heritage.

> WENDI
> Okay, but the Alamo wasn't . . .

> MOM ON LEFT
> Isn't that spatula set adorable?

OPEN on a dark parking lot at 5:30 a.m. A group of women in various sizes and states of shape sloppily do push-ups on yoga mats while a buff Texas woman named Mandy blows a whistle and screams, "COME ON, LADIES! TEN MORE! BELIEVE IN YOURSELVES!" and Shakira's "Hips Don't Lie" blasts on a boombox.

> WENDI
> I didn't . . . think Boot Camp . . . for Women would be so . . . intense.

JOCK MOM

Gotta keep our booties tight for our hubbies! Oh, cheese and crackers! Are you puking? Coach Mandy! Wendi's puking!

OPEN on a class party. The room is festively covered in (non-religious) winter décor and there's a table loaded with (non-allergen) food and drinks. A CD of seasonal music brightly plays, and the kids run around happily. Reluctant Room Mom WENDI, dressed in an obligatory red sweater, stands to the side and watches the scene with relief. She can't believe she actually pulled this event off, considering her lack of hostess and organizational skills. And her deep-seated fear of Party City. But while she's proud she did it, she also feels embarrassed that this is her only accomplishment lately. And then she feels shame about the embarrassment because what kind of person isn't happy that she gets to do something like arrange a party for kids? She's clearly a mess. She leaves the room and walks into the hallway for some fresh air, but then she's shocked to overhear two moms whispering . . . about her? What the hell? Did she just walk through a portal to 1986? She ducks behind a papier-mâché snowman to eavesdrop.

MOM 1

Seriously, can you believe that she didn't even
bother to bring a chocolate fountain? It's not a party
without a chocolate fountain. Everyone knows that.

MOM 2

I know! I feel so bad for our kiddos! We totally
need to make sure one of us is Room Mom next year
so Wendi doesn't do it again. This was a *disaster*.

Shaken but also perversely delighted, if she's being honest, Wendi stays hidden until they leave. It's definitely a blow to be insulted like that, but what's worse is that two meanies named Ashley gossiping about her is the only palace intrigue available in her life right now. She really thought she'd be involved in at least a few tawdry celebrity scandals by this point. What's next, humiliation from the crossing guard? But later that week, an unexpected ally arises when the class teacher gives Wendi a holiday gift of a wine bottle stopper with the note, "Happy Holidays. Figured you could use this."

OPEN on a movie theater. A row of suburban women sit together, eagerly waiting for *Twilight* to begin. A couple of women sip the wine they smuggled into the theater via their purses. Wendi is kind of happy to be there because she'll go anywhere for popcorn, even into a war zone, but she is also troubled because she's at a teenage vampire film.

WENDI

(to mom on her right)
Psst, when I joined this book club, I thought we'd
be reading books. Like ones for grown-ups. Not going
to movies.

MOM ON RIGHT

Nope, this is easier. And they're shirtless! Go
#TEAMJACOB!

So obviously Mom Prom was a bust. Not only did I not even get to first base, I pretty much had a wrist corsage shoved in my face. It was one bucket of pig's blood short of *Carrie*. There was nothing wrong with any of those women—besides the Confederate flag asshole and the climate change deniers—they just weren't *my* women.

The only things we had in common were our neighborhood, our school, and the fact that we'd reproduced around the same time. They weren't interesting people to me, and I clearly wasn't interesting to them. Which, of course, was my own fault because I wasn't showing them my interesting parts. I was showing them my Great Mom parts. I didn't even blame Texas for this because it could have happened to me in the hippest neighborhood in Brooklyn or the fanciest school in Paris too. Clicking with other parents is a matter of luck, and I didn't have much. I felt like the Odd Woman Out once again.

My loneliness from not finding my mom group and my pathological need to be liked then compelled me to do something rash: I volunteered to be the PTO's communications officer. Yes, that's right, OFFICER, even though nobody would give me a badge when I repeatedly asked at the front desk. Because I wasn't skilled enough for an executive office, like president or carnival director, I was put in charge of the monthly school newsletter. A heady responsibility. "I'm finally writing!" I told myself, even though all I wrote was news you can use about third grade fundraisers and the ongoing head lice epidemic. It wasn't the best use of my skills, to say the least, but my time in office showed me how some women get their start in politics from the PTO because, much like Washington, D.C., it was a little cutthroat. One week, I forgot to include something a PTO Big Wig had sent me for the newsletter, and suddenly I was Michael Douglas in *Fatal Attraction* just trying to not get stabbed on my way to the after-school pick-up zone. The Big Wig sent me angry emails and left angry voicemails and said passive-aggressive things to me in our board meeting like, "Do you want me to repeat that so this time you remember to include something I said in the newsletter?" Thank god none of the classes had pet rabbits that year.

"This is my life now," I thought while I nonchalantly listened to her chastise me on another day. "Harassed by a middle-aged woman with chunky highlights, adult braces, and a son named Maverick because I didn't include a blurb about the Cub Scouts popcorn sale in the school newsletter. It's fine. Everything's fine. I am *thriving*."

What had happened to the confident adult I thought I'd grown into? Why was I in my forties, yet navigating this pseudo–high school world feeling like a clueless sixteen-year-old again? I couldn't even stand up to a bully in an ugly skort when I'd once deftly handled Hollywood producers. Okay, somewhat deftly, let's be honest. I cried a few times in the ladies' room. But clearly, being a grade-school parent had made me regress, big time. Are you there, God? It's me, Wendi, and nobody likes me. I know that's Judy Blume and not the John Hughes metaphor I've ineptly been trying to make work this whole time, but the point is that I was a sad loser with nothing left to hope for but a watery death in the school carnival dunk tank.

But then came my Molly Ringwald moment. My triumphant slow-motion walk into the third act of Mom Prom while "If You Leave" by Orchestral Manoeuvres in the Dark blasts on the soundtrack, and I slyly smile at my haters while wearing an okay-we-now-realize-it-was-kind-of-ugly handmade pink dress.

After a hellacious flight to Nevada to visit my parents for Christmas, complete with weather delays, two antsy kids, and painful menstrual cramps, I staggered into a stall in the restroom at the Reno airport and opened up an Always maxi-pad. And there, while industrial toilets flushed and fluorescent lights blinked and nearby slot machines dinged, I looked at the sticker on the maxi-pad and saw these four condescending words: "Have a Happy Period." I knew I'd just struck gold. I didn't know that gold would change my life's direction. Hey, not everyone's light bulb scene looks like something from a gauzy Merchant Ivory film. Some of us have our watershed moment standing next to a public toilet that smells like cigarettes.

Inspired by a category called "An Open Letter to People or Entities Who Are Unlikely to Respond" on the humor website McSweeney's, I spent the next two months writing an angry and funny letter to a fictional product manager at Procter & Gamble regarding their use of the "Have a Happy Period" slogan. I emailed my missive to the editor and nervously waited to hear back. I was thrilled when they accepted it, and it ran on their main page for maybe three days. Their small, niche audience read it, as did Chris and the few friends in LA I emailed it to, and I thought that was it. Just a feather in my nonexistent writing career cap that I soon forgot about. Until it changed everything.

Many things go viral now, but not a lot did back in 2008. The Always letter not only went viral, it went *looney nutso viral*. This was a couple years before Twitter even existed, so it ricocheted around the world via people copying, pasting, and emailing it, or snail mailing it, or posting it on blogs or in chat rooms. There wasn't as much outraged feminist humor writing online back then, so my satirical stand against the patriarchy struck a nerve and took on a life of its own. Some people claimed the letter was real (it was not); others claimed that it was "*PC Magazine*'s Editor's Choice for Best Letter" (it was not). I heard about that one when my nerdy neighbor knocked on the door to tell me, "I just read about you on Snopes! I had no idea you were funny!" Because my email address was findable via my McSweeney's bio, my inbox soon filled up with praise, anger, thank-yous, and detailed stories about various women's personal menstruation journeys. So many uterine stories. So many.

My letter was reprinted in a major San Francisco newspaper and in more than a few non-major newspapers. One day, I answered an unknown number on my phone and two morning shock jock DJs from a radio station in West Virginia screamed, "We're live on air with the angry period woman! Are you ANGREEEEEE?!?" I hung up. But perhaps the weirdest moment was during my annual exam at my OB/GYN's office when I was on the exam table, a giant paper napkin covering my privates, and looked up to see my work posted on the wall. "There's your letter! We're all so proud of you!" my doctor said. "Now get ready because this is going to be a little cold." David Sedaris probably hasn't ever read his own humor writing while his feet are up in stirrups.

I've forgotten a lot of the letter hoopla but I know that a high school theater team performed it in a state competition and won. So did a Canadian beauty pageant contestant. A few people made videos of themselves acting it out, which was strange and wonderful to watch. I was offered representation, friendship, marriage, grisly death, and more than a few lifetime supplies of "alternative feminine hygiene products." (Enough already, Diva Cup.) To this day, my mom carries a dog-eared copy of the letter in her purse to show off to cruise ship passengers and grocery cashiers. "Oh, you just *have* to read what my daughter wrote about periods. Caution: she really likes the f-word!"

But here's the weird thing: while all of this was happening, I still didn't mention it at the grade school or to any of the other moms in my neighborhood. I was proud of it for sure, but because the letter is a little R-rated, I thought it best to stay quiet. I kept that part of my life private. I now realize that some of them must have known about it because it was everywhere, but nobody said a word. Who knows, maybe I should have mentioned it and glommed onto the people who liked it and saved myself a lot of loneliness.

More than ten years after the letter originally ran on McSweeney's, Benedict Cumberbatch's stage show *Letters Live* somehow found it, and it's now been performed in London by comedian and showrunner Sharon Horgan and in New York by Emmy-winner Uzo Aduba. Actress Alison Brie read it at the Net-a-Porter Hollywood Women gala to a roomful of A-list actresses, and it was a big hit, even though I'm guessing most have never been inside a Reno airport bathroom. Their loss.

None of that really mattered to me, though. What mattered was that the Always letter showed me that I was able to write humor and reach people with it. I could sit at my little makeshift desk in my bedroom and be the funny, snarky person I wasn't in my day-to-day life when I was trying to be a Great or at least Good Mom. The letter's success compelled me to start a blog in 2009 so I could keep writing and expressing myself in ways I clearly wasn't doing in person. The moms at school didn't see my real personality, which was by design and maybe a mistake on my part, but what was stopping me from showing myself to the rest of the world? While hoping none of the moms at school found out about it? Keeping my Blogspot.com blog on the downlow goes against everything today's writers are told about "building your platform."

The "They're Not All Gems"-subtitled blog WendiAarons.com had a few readers to start, then a few more, and a few more. I'd post short, humorous things, mostly about parenting because that was my life. It scratched the creative itch in my brain, and most essential, it was something that was just for me. But then something amazing happened. Other funny women and moms from around the country liked my writing and my sense of humor, and they left comments saying just that. I'd click on their names and visit their blogs, and I liked them and their senses of humor too. We soon formed a little online group, and we'd read and comment on each other's blogs every week. Suddenly it didn't matter that I wasn't brave enough to be my real self at the kids' school because I found another place I could do it. I found other women to laugh with me, not at me. I became friends with a lawyer in Manhattan, and a former sales director in Madison, and a mom of two who used to be a news anchor in Connecticut. On the internet, I wasn't "Sam's mom" or "Jack's mom" or "the mom who brought Oreos and expired string cheese for the soccer game snack." I was "that angry period lady" and "a super funny writer."

The Always letter was my first foray into using humor to help me make sense of the world. Satire became my way to process and express my anger or confusion or disgust with various topics like aging or prejudice or politics or sexism. It's a great coping mechanism. As my first favorite saying goes, "Don't get mad, get funny," and my second favorite saying goes, "Humor is a rubber sword. It allows you to make a point without drawing blood."

So what that I didn't remember that stupid chocolate fountain, or the stupid Cub Scout popcorn news? And so what that I didn't like books about teenage vampires or doing squats at 5:30 a.m. to keep myself attractive to my husband? Yes, I was spectacularly bad at cutting out shapes from construction paper, and yes, my twinset had a few stains on it because I fell asleep watching *Apocalypse Now* with a taco in my hand, but who cared? Why was I trying to be a Great Mom at the expense of being a Real Mom? Because of that humble little maxi-pad I opened in the Reno airport bathroom that year, my life changed. I learned that if I put myself out there via my writing and my humor and my feminist passion, I'd find the friends I wanted. I'd be happier because my identity was no longer only a stay-at-home mom. The time had come for me to graduate from high school for the second time and walk away with my head held high.

Cue OMD.

AN OPEN LETTER TO MR. JAMES THATCHER, BRAND MANAGER, PROCTER & GAMBLE

Dear Mr. Thatcher,

I have been a loyal user of your Always maxi-pads for over 20 years, and I appreciate many of their features. Why, without the LeakGuard Core™ or Dri-Weave™ absorbency, I'd probably never go horseback riding or salsa dancing, and I'd certainly steer clear of running up and down the beach in tight, white shorts. But my favorite feature has to be your revolutionary Flexi-Wings. Kudos on being the only company smart enough to realize how crucial it is that maxi-pads be aerodynamic. I can't tell you how safe and secure I feel each month knowing there's a little F-16 in my pants.

Have you ever had a menstrual period, Mr. Thatcher? Ever suffered from "the curse"? I'm guessing you haven't. Well, my "time of the month" is starting right now. As I type, I can already feel hormonal forces violently surging through my body. Just a few minutes from now, my body will adjust and I'll be transformed into what my husband likes to call "an inbred hillbilly with knife skills." Isn't the human body amazing?

As brand manager in the feminine-hygiene division, you've no doubt seen quite a bit of research on what exactly happens during your customers' monthly visits from Aunt Flo. Therefore, you must know about the bloating, puffiness, and cramping we endure, and about our intense mood swings, crying jags, and out-of-control behavior. You surely realize it's a tough time for most women. In fact, only last week, my friend Jennifer fought the violent urge to shove her boyfriend's testicles into a George Foreman Grill just because he told her he thought *Grey's Anatomy* was written by drunken squirrels. Crazy! The point is, sir, you of all people must realize that America is just crawling with homicidal maniacs in capri pants. Which brings me to the reason for my letter.

Last month, while in the throes of cramping so painful I wanted to reach inside my body and yank out my uterus, I opened an Always maxi-pad, and there, printed on the adhesive backing, were these words: "Have a Happy Period."

Are you fucking kidding me?

What I mean is, does any part of your tiny middle-manager brain really think happiness—actual smiling, laughing happiness—is possible during a menstrual period? Did anything mentioned above sound the least bit pleasurable? Well, did it, James? FYI, unless you're some kind of professional masochist, there will never be anything "happy" about a day in which you have to jack yourself up on Motrin and Kahlúa and lock yourself in your house just so you don't march down to the local Walgreens armed with a shiv made out of an eyelash curler and a sketchy plan to take a hostage in the Incontinence aisle. For the love of God, pull your head out, man. If you just have to slap a moronic message on a maxi-pad, wouldn't it make more sense to say something that's actually pertinent, like "Put Down the Hammer" or "Vehicular Manslaughter Is Wrong"? Or are you just picking on us?

Sir, please inform your accounting department that, effective immediately, there will be an $8 drop in monthly profits, for I have chosen to take my maxi-pad business elsewhere. And though I will certainly miss your Flexi-Wings, I will not for one minute miss your brand of condescending bullshit. And that's a promise I will keep. Always.

Best,
Wendi Aarons
Austin, TX

CHAPTER FOUR

I'M WEARING CONFERENCE SWAG NOW

The first time I saw a naked woman descend a two-story escalator, I was in Chicago. "Maybe that's why it's called the Windy City," I quipped to the other women in the hotel lobby, like I was Dorothy Parker sipping dry martinis at the Algonquin Round Table instead of a middle-aged mom slugging back room-temperature chardonnay at a blogging conference. "Looks like *someone* could use one of those nice Sheraton robes that I stuffed into my suitcase right about now."

I was only acting blasé about Naked Jen, as I'd soon learn she was called, because that wasn't the only odd occurrence I'd seen that day. Or that hour. Right before the slow-moving public nudity happened, I'd been in the conference's bustling exhibit hall that featured over a hundred sponsor booths, all of them gifting bloggers with free swag. Everything from jars of baby food to memory sticks to Jimmy Dean Sausage alarm clocks was available to grab and plop into your bulging conference tote bag. I found it overwhelming and overstimulating, but I was in the minority. Brands were working overtime to make an impression on the internet's proto influencers, and the influencers were hoping to build relationships with companies that would pay to sponsor their blogs. Or at least give them something to take home to their kids as payment for leaving to spend time with their online friends. "Sorry you had to deal with daddy all weekend, but here's a jar of artisanal sauerkraut to enjoy, Jagger!"

On our way out of the exhibit hall that day, my funny and sarcastic friend Mariana and I passed a gaggle of women crowding around one particular booth like seagulls fighting over a saltine. "What's going on over there?" I asked while we watched one woman hip check another, then flail her arms like she was trying to catch a fly ball at a Dodgers game. Mariana was, and is, one of my good friends, both in the blogosphere and out. We met after she left funny comments on my blog posts, and I left, in my opinion, even funnier ones on hers. I've visited her in NYC a few times and stayed at her West Village apartment, something I couldn't have imagined when I first started a humor blog from my Texas bedroom because nobody in my neighborhood liked me.

"That insanity over there is the Trojan booth," Mariana said in her deadpan Russian accent, accompanied by an eye roll. "It's always a mob scene." Then, noticing my confusion as to why a group of women at a blogging conference that had .002 percent male attendees would need packs of condoms, she explained. "They've been handing out free vibrators all day. So good fucking luck to the TSA agents at O'Hare when everyone flies home on Sunday. Most of the luggage will be buzzing."

"That's wild," I muttered, but then, never one to back away from a challenge, I shoved my tote bag at her, ran over to the rowdy crowd and used the childhood skills I gained from chasing Blue Light Specials at Kmart to worm my way into the melee and triumphantly grab two Trojan Vibrations. They're still in the top of my closet, next to my novelty sweaters. Pink, new in package, vintage 2009 vibrators. Make me an offer, priority shipping included.

I knew from the moment I saw women scream their blog names—"OH MY GOD, YOU'RE VODKA MOM! I'M FULL

FAT YOGURT MOM!"—and latch onto each other like lobsters that BlogHer 2009 would be unlike anything I'd ever experienced. And I spent four squeeful years in a sorority house for some godforsaken reason. But girls gone wild on spring break are nothing compared to grown women gone wild on a break from their ordinary lives and families. It was like our Mardi Gras. Most of us had left behind the demands of our houses, partners, kids, jobs, and pets for a weekend spent on just our own interests. It felt indulgent. Luxurious. We had major Mom Guilt too, of course, but it was easy to get over that when there was swag and wild dance parties and an exciting city and so many new people to meet and befriend. Like me, my group of blog friends felt like they'd been stuck at home for years, trapped in the trenches of mommyland with zero mental stimulation. This feeling was the main reason most of us started writing in the first place. We wanted to connect, find our community, be known as someone other than "So-and-so's mom," and use our voices in ways we maybe didn't or couldn't IRL. We wanted to be heard and now, in the packed hotel lobby, to be seen.

Well, heard and seen right after we stood in line for thirty minutes to get a photo with Caitlyn Jenner, years before she transitioned, as part of the Tropicana booth's "Juice with Bruce" promotion. (Side note: How lazy was the marketing person who said, "Fuck it, 'juice' rhymes with 'Bruce', get me Jenner on the phone"?)

I'd met a few bloggers in person before that first conference but not many. Meeting someone in real life after chatting online wasn't as common back then. I've never even done any online dating because it didn't exist when I was single. I met Chris the old-fashioned way: standing next to the keg at a Reno fraternity party in a giant rugby shirt, belting off-key Tom Petty before vomiting Zima on a boombox. No swiping right needed when you have that much sex appeal! But not only was it still awkward to meet people who read your blog in the early 2000s, it even held a whiff of danger. Like the first time I had coffee with another Austin blogger—as soon as I walked up to her, she nervously giggled and said, "I feel that you should know that my husband's waiting in the car in case you turn out to be an axe murderer."

"Oh!" I answered, a little insulted. "Well, kindly tell your husband that A) I don't have the upper arm strength to hold an axe much less decapitate you with it and B) My husband is also very concerned that I'm meeting an internet stranger which is why he yelled, 'What should I feed the boys for dinner if you end up strangled in a quarry?' when I left. Wow, you look a lot bigger than your avatar."

Over time it became less awkward to take friendships from online to offline, and the conferences made it happen on steroids. BlogHer was started by three women in Silicon Valley who saw that the burgeoning blog movement was mostly women trying to find a way to connect with each other, so they formed an online community that became famous for its annual in-person event. It was a hugely anticipated weekend, with thousands of attendees, hundreds of sponsors, and speakers on everything from monetizing your blog to the best way to photograph food to "what should I do if my mother-in-law reads what I write about her online?" (Answer: write about her in a journal with a lock on it, dummy.) The conference sessions and keynote speeches were mostly business-focused, despite what my story about the exhibit hall would lead you to believe. It was at these conferences that I learned what SEO, algorithm, online footprint, and other terms that hurt my brain meant. The women who were online back then truly were digital pioneers. That includes the actual Pioneer Woman, Ree Drummond, who was at those early conferences as a new blogger, along with other future superstars like Glennon Doyle, Luvvie Ajayi, and Jenny Lawson. One year, Jenny and I spoke on a panel about humor blogging, and she wore her long, red "confidence wig" that made her look like a wasted mermaid. Now, she's a bookstore owner and best-selling author—I'm not entirely sure what the wig is up to these days.

The somewhat radical idea of women, most of them moms, gathering because we were speaking out and writing about our ordinary lives was so new and strange back then that local TV stations would often send a crew to cover it—usually with a big whiff of condescension. "Mommy bloggers are in town this weekend, but this time they're not swapping recipes, they're swapping business tips! Let's talk to a few who hope to support their family with their blogs, haha!" Can you imagine anyone covering any gathering of men in that way? "Insurance agents are here in Pittsburgh for their annual conference, but these men are a lot more than just blobby dad bods giving away free pens!" Even furry conventions where grown-ass adults have sex in animal costumes get more respect than we did.

The conferences could be overwhelming with so many people, and I confess that I didn't really know the term "introvert" before I started blogging. The words "shy" or "private" were more often used to describe someone who had limits to their socializing. But I soon found out that many of the attendees at BlogHer were self-proclaimed introverts who expressed themselves best online. The woman who left the funniest comments on your blog may turn out to be super quiet in person. I totally understood that and have been confronted about my obnoxious online voice not matching my more chill in-person voice more than a few times. (Let's be real, though, if I was actually like my online voice in real life, you would hate me within ten seconds, guaranteed.) I wasn't sure what category I was in then, but now I've taken enough online personality quizzes to consider myself an introverted extroverted Enneagram nine Scorpio INTF Princess

Jasmine. Okay, that's not true but I do know that extrovert or not, it was a lot easier to say "Good god, was *Fifty Shades of Grey* written by a woman who just learned the alphabet the day before, or should we blame a team of meth monkeys for this travesty?" on my blog than say it in person to a mom from school who then started crying because that book trilogy really meant a lot to her. (True story. Hope you're doing okay, Pam.)

I tried for years to find my place with the mom crowd at school, but I already had my friend group in place when I showed up at that first conference. Mariana and Kelcey and Ann and Lisa, just to name a few. My little group of humor writing weirdos who related to the funny part of me that I was just starting to recognize and develop. We'd been commenting and emailing and talking on the phone for months, so by the time we finally met in real life, it was like we'd known each other forever. Any awkwardness disappeared within minutes because we felt like we really knew each other's lives by reading about them. Maybe the reason I like watching *90 Day Fiancé* so much is because it reminds me of those early days when I found my soulmates, but because of distance, we had to stay in touch like lovelorn pen pals and only see each other once or twice a year. Or maybe I just like that show because it's fun to watch grizzled fifty-year-old American women hook up with twenty-five-year-old Jamaican resort hotties who have sex with them in exchange for fancy watches, and I'm putting that plan in my back pocket should I ever need it. (In fact, I'm currently in a *90 Day Fiancé* text group with three of my old-school blogger friends that is *highly* entertaining.)

Perhaps the biggest gift the BlogHer conferences gave me, as a resident of a homogenous Texas neighborhood, was diversity. Diversity in all ways. Gender identity, sexual orientation, race, ethnicity, moms of all kinds, people with disabilities, and even a Wiccan or two. You name a type of person, and I can bet you they were at the conferences using their voices to connect with others. I met people at the conferences that I'd *never* meet in my cul-de-sac. Maybe not even in Austin. I'm truly grateful for that because engaging with all kinds of people and hearing their stories opened up my world in a huge way. It helped me become aware of injustices and missions and celebrations that permanently changed my thinking. Thank god for that because I couldn't take another night of listening to updates on Ethan's rash at Bunco night. Will his psoriasis *ever* clear up?

Back to the digital pioneer thing: Gen X doesn't get enough credit for having one foot in analog and one foot in digital. We grew up with rotary phones, for fuck's sake. We had to get up off the couch to change the stupid channel on the stupid TV set and then the show that was on was probably something starring Gabe Kaplan and a chimp. I remember my family feeling like *The Jetsons* when we finally got a push-button phone in 1982. I thought of that old Trimline during a BlogHer 2009 session when a speaker was explaining a big, new social media thing to all of us called a "hashtag."

"It's just a dumb pound sign with words behind it," the scowling food blogger next to me whispered when she noticed my confused face. "For example, right now I'm using the hashtag 'pound sign areyoufuckingkiddingmewiththisshit' but only in my head because I'm an introverted extrovert." I confess that I didn't understand social media at all at the time, but most everyone else in the room did because they were tech savvy and eager to be early adopters. Even those who were born in the (gasp) '60s. Later that night, though, we all got a lesson on exactly what hashtags were and how they could be used for both #good and #evil.

The Nikon brand representatives were in Chicago that weekend to court and meet mom bloggers, and they threw an invite-only, non–

conference sanctioned party at a swanky downtown bar. Exclusive events like this always caused hurt feelings when you didn't make the guest list, which I hadn't. But Mariana's blog was big enough, so I went along with her as her plus-one, a fact that she lorded over me all night. "Will you get me a refill, Plus-One? I think I'm a little warm, Plus-One. Can you fan me and maybe bring me a salad? You know, because I'm the hero that was invited to this party. Thank you, glommer-onner!"

Celebrities were often hired for these influencer events to add some glamour, and the one we got that night was Carson Kressley from the original *Queer Eye for the Straight Guy*. He was stationed near a backdrop and klieg light setup and tasked with helping bloggers pose for a pic taken by a photographer with a Nikon. Maybe he was nice to the first one-hundred people who came by, but by the time I got to him he was over the lady blogger shit. Really over it. I looked into his face, which was covered in some kind of pancake foundation that I probably couldn't afford, and nervously told him, "I'm not very photogenic." Which is true. I look like Dog the Bounty Hunter's mugshot in most of my grade school photos. Instead of taking that into consideration, however, Carson ignored my worries and breezily said, "Oh, honey. I can make anyone look good." No doubt thinking of all the guys on his show that he'd transformed from schlubby Midwestern man into schlubby Midwestern man but with hair gel. He sharply instructed me to lift my chin, turn to the left, suck it in, and "tszuj" which I still don't know how to do or spell, and I ended up performing an uncoordinated and awkward robot dance like a background extra in *Breakin' 2: Electric Boogaloo*. Then I froze my face in a smile, waited for the flash, and two seconds later we both leaned into the monitor to see the promised results. "Well, looks like you were right," Carson grimaced. "Next!"

Queer Eye for the Wend-i: coming soon to nowhere near you.

But what that party is legendary for isn't my complete humiliation at the callous hands of Carson Kressley. The legend goes that a blogger tried to enter the bar with her baby, and the young PR woman running the guest list that night wouldn't let her in. Because she had A. Baby. In. A. Bar. (Where my *Sweet Home Alabama* fans at?) It was pretty much a non-story until a conference attendee decided to stir some shit and use her new hashtag knowledge to post #NikonHatesBabies on Twitter as a joke. It was kind of funny and harmless, but then all hell broke loose when the hashtag unexpectedly took off. Soon a lot of people were tweeting #NikonHatesBabies for no real reason but to join in. It was definitely attention-getting, though. So much so that the next day Nikon executives flew into town for some crisis brand management, and the baby-denying PR guest-list woman was even seen crying in the elevator. Oops. I hope she got another job that doesn't involve social media. Or babies.

The lesson from Nikongate was that suddenly anyone with a computer and Wi-Fi could be heard. Even us boring-ass *moms*. So what if you were a SAHM, you could still be relevant if you had a computer. This was still a few years before Zuckerberg really entered the chat and fucked up everyone's family Thanksgivings until the end of time, and years before everyone's grandma was posting racist shit on Pinterest, so it felt revolutionary and empowering to us. We realized that we could now amplify each other's voices and talk about what was important to us, be it racial equity or movie reviews or recipes. We were able to both shrink and expand our worlds via our online communities. Early blogging communities were the precursor to today's social media–organized social justice marches and rallies for reproductive and voting rights, and to support the #MeToo movement and the Black Lives Matter movement. So while some bloggers may have been a little too hashtag happy that night, overall I think these communities have been a force for good—certainly in my life.

Let me state for the record: Nikon doesn't hate babies.

Carson Kressley might.

I attended about six BlogHer conferences in all, and I also started attending a smaller, similar conference run by my friend Laura called Mom 2.0 where one year I won the Iris Award for Most Entertaining (#humblebrag) and got my photo taken with Andrew Shue from *Melrose Place*. These weekends away became my time to be around people who really understood me. I mean, besides Chris, of course. Speaking of my husband, he was always supportive of me going to the conferences because he saw how much happier I was when I came home. How much more fulfilled. The conferences and blogging empowered me to discover another part of myself, a creative part, that wasn't about my kids, or him, or my parents, or the drama of the school PTO. It was something that was just for me.

A lot of people back then called this experience finally finding their "tribe," which is an indigenous word we should no longer use in that context (see also: spirit animal). But the internet, for all its faults like filters that make everyone look like deer and its contribution to the collapse of democracy, gave us a way to find where we fit in. It gave women who were isolated in their communities a way to feel less lonely. The conferences were a bit like summer camp in that regard. Once or twice a year, you packed your suitcase, left town, and let your freak flag fly with your crew. And fly it did.

One year at a hotel in Florida, my nerd herd decided to reenact the opening scene from *Friends* in the fancy marble fountain. Yes, we had been drinking. The front desk person didn't think to wonder why we asked to borrow six umbrellas on a clear night, but maybe she should have after we started jumping around like Joey, Chandler, and

Monica, yelling, "We don't care if you don't like it!" at the table of finance bros that told us to shut up. Another year, someone sent hotel security to our room because we were singing Dolly Parton's "Jolene" a little too loudly and a few too many times. While my friend Lisa sat quietly on the bed and the rest of us hid behind the door like middle-age delinquents, my rather sophisticated friend Nancy, who has an MBA, a published book, and a serious job, tipsily greeted the guard by asking, "Eees there a pwoblem, offica?" We were 100 percent the people I call the front desk to complain about, but it felt amazing to be immature and irresponsible for once. It's even more fun when deep down you know you shouldn't act that way because you're "of a certain age" and you do it anyway. But why give up that joy just because you're no longer twenty? Plus, if worse comes to worst, we're all old enough to afford bail and a good lawyer.

I knew that my adult life was lacking friends that felt like family, but I didn't know how much until those women came into my life via my blog's URL. The Mom Prom wasn't a good fit for me *at all*, but this group was. Maybe because the safety of the computer allowed me to finally show my whole self. Hands down, starting to write, finding my voice, and then finding my group was the best thing to happen to me in my forties. Even better than the day I saw my PTO rival fall down a small flight of stairs. (She was *fine*.) If you can find friends in your neighborhood who make you happy, that's great. It saves a lot of time and money spent on airfare. But if not, if you just don't fit in no matter how hard you try, keep looking. There's no age limit to making a friend. There's no quantity limit to how many people you might connect with. They're out there. Maybe one is waiting in line for a free vibrator right this minute.

On the last day of my first BlogHer in Chicago in 2009, I stood in the back of the big stage that was set up in a ballroom, holding two wrinkled pieces of paper in my hand and trying my best to not throw up. A blog post of mine had been selected as one of the ten "Voices of the Year" winners, and I was about to read my writing to a room of three-thousand people, including famous editor Tina Brown—a big ask of someone who hadn't been on stage since she starred as Abraham Lincoln in the second-grade school play because she was the tallest kid in the class. I was still seriously considering bowing out, and almost went to the organizer to say, "I can't do this. I'm too scared." But then I heard the other women and men who were picked to read that day. Some of their stories were about deeply personal issues, like adoption and tragedy and loss, and I realized that I had to just get over myself and be brave. My story was my story, and my essay's subject ("I Love Diet Coke") was ridiculous compared to their subjects—like really ridiculous, like who the hell writes a love letter to Diet Coke? But still. I wrote something good enough to be acknowledged by my peers, and I needed to honor that. I needed to stop being quiet in the corner and step loudly into the spotlight. I'd just started figuring out who I was, and maybe it was this: a person that celebrated her wins.

"Our next Voice of the Year is Wendi Aarons!" the emcee boomed into the microphone. With my knees shaking, and my pulse racing, and my dress from Marshalls (*never* Ross Dress for Less) gathering flop sweat, I staggered my way onto center stage. My hands gripped the podium, and I looked into the audience that was filled with people rooting for me to do well. Well, maybe a few weren't because I stole their Trojan Vibrations, but they were all waiting to hear what I had to say, which had never happened to me before in my entire life. I took a deep breath, put a smile on my face, hoped my quaking legs weren't visible to the crowd, and then I seized the damn moment and I killed it.

You know how everyone says you should picture the audience in their underwear when you're nervous about public speaking? I pictured them all naked on a two-story escalator.

CHAPTER FIVE

I'M WEARING BAD DECISIONS FROM THE JUNIORS DEPARTMENT NOW

I had a midlife crisis in a Dillard's. I would have preferred my public breakdown to have taken place somewhere a little more upscale, like a Nordstrom or maybe even a Neiman Marcus, but a mid-priced Texas department store with bad lighting and a teenage shoplifting problem was probably more fitting. Plus, now I know to never sob in the Reba section because they get a little touchy if you wipe your tears on one of Reba's kicky faux-suede fringe jackets. Here's your one chance, Fancy, don't let me down, indeed.

It's weird to be in your mid-forties. Let me rephrase that. It's *fucking weird* to be in your mid-forties. You're not exactly old, but you're not young, either. And maybe you're not quite ready to call yourself middle-aged, but that's how everyone else in the world would describe you in a police report. "Yes, officer, the lady I saw flipping off Governor Greg Abbott's motorcade while chugging white wine out of a Ziploc gallon bag was *definitely* middle-aged." Unfortunately, the phrase is accurate because forty is generally considered the halfway mark in life. I'm sure some of us wish that middle age wasn't until sixty, but come on. Who the hell wants to live to be one hundred twenty these days? Especially if you own ocean-front property.

By the time I hit forty-five, I was finally coming out of my mom fog. Sam and Jack had survived their early childhood, and surprisingly, so had I. We were in the sweet end-of-grade-school years, and I could once again focus on myself a little. That was a positive thing, but I soon noticed that I'd lost a little fashion footing in my time spent chained to the oven all day. I was one homemade prairie dress away from Kimmy Schmidt after she escaped the bunker. Not exactly a mole woman, but I was definitely reentering the world with some growing pains. Specifically, wardrobe-wise. I didn't know what to wear. Or what not to wear. Or what to want to wear if I could pull it off without full-body liposuction and/or a whale-bone corset from ye olden times. I had absolutely no style identity besides "tornado survivor."

Thanks to my emerging writing career and going to conferences and other events, I finally felt like I was more than just a mother, but I also wasn't a career professional. I didn't care if I looked sexy, but I also didn't want to look like a massive hosebeast. I would never wear low-rise jeans, but I sure as hell wouldn't wear those god-awful mom jeans embedded with nanotechnology to make my stomach one inch smaller, either. Sweatpants? Too sloppy. Dresses? Too fancy. Holiday-themed appliqued sweaters? Back off, man. I'm not teaching kindergarten in Denmark. After a few weeks spent crying in my closet because I couldn't find anything to wear, I wondered if I should just join a cult because at least then my wardrobe choices would be easy: A) a white robe or B) a different white robe. True, I'd be required to have tons of cult sex with The Master, but maybe the thigh rashes and permanent brainwashing would be worth it to never enter a TJ Maxx again.

It wasn't just confusion about my role in life giving me what to wear problems, either. I had no idea how to dress for my age. "You're *forty-five*" would pop into my head whenever I went clothes shopping. I didn't know what was appropriate for my age, and Banana Republic doesn't have a "Too Old for Booty Shorts, Too Young for Depends" section. There's no "Midlife Writer Chicks" tab on Shein.com. That said, what does "dressing for your age" even mean anymore? What even is "age appropriate"? We're mostly past that kind of determination as a society by now, I think. Women's magazines cashed in on judgmental aging and fashion tips for years, but now any online outlet that dares post "the best outfits for women over forty" is immediately attacked by an outraged public screaming, "Just because I have an AARP card doesn't mean I can't wear a crop top, *motherfucker*. SUCK IT, OPRAH. COM." Which I totally agree with—death to the patriarchy, stop the body shaming, free the cellulite, and all that—but also: what *are* the best outfits for women over forty because I have no fucking idea.

What Not to Wear If You're Over Forty

1. Whimsical rainbow suspenders
2. An Oregon Ducks mascot costume
3. A look of willingness at a PTO meeting
4. White pants after Labor Day—and by Labor Day, I mean the day you were in labor
5. Any lingerie crocheted by the Amish
6. Your teen daughter's shirt (only because of the ensuing drama)
7. Pleated khakis
8. Your prom dress, especially if it's Gunne Sax or Laura Ashley

Alternate list:

What to Wear If You're Over Forty

1. Whatever the hell you want so you can squeeze a *modicum* of joy out of this pathetic existence.

Some people's style gets stuck in the era of their life that they most enjoyed, and that seems like an appealing and easy choice. Like the old dudes who still look like they're dealing drugs under a San Diego boardwalk in 1977: bell bottoms, sideburns, feathered hair, gold medallion around the neck, usually named "Dusty" or "Rusty." We've all seen Rusty working the door at a classic rock concert, or maybe Dusty sold you some weed once or twice (if so, I hope you enjoyed smoking oregano and lawn clippings). There are also the women who found their favorite hairstyle in 1950 and refuse to modernize their shellacked hair helmet. That's a common sight in certain parts of "the higher the hair, the closer to God" rural Texas, and I always get worried when I see those ladies standing near a ceiling fan in a BBQ restaurant. "Back it up, Bunny Sue and Bobby Sue! Y'all is fixin' to get snatched up by the demon rotors!" I briefly considered returning to my '80s look because I did enjoy the '80s, mostly because I was in college and usually drunk, but I decided it'd be too much work. I'd have to get a perm and scour low-rent thrift shops for shoulder-padded blazers worn by the casts of *Who's the Boss?* and *Working Girl.* And stone-washed stirrup jeans are harder to come by than you'd think.

By my mid-forties I'd at least gotten rid of the infamous mom haircut and twinsets that made me look like a sitcom wife named Deb. This was much to Chris's relief. "It's so strange because you *look* like the type of person who knows how to cook, and yet you *don't* know how to cook!" he once said in wonder. I couldn't even take it as an insult because it was the day after I'd used Montreal Steak Seasoning as a steak rub instead of a steak sprinkle, and we had to throw away thirty dollars' worth of meat because it would have sent us to the hospital with salt poisoning. He, of course, has never had style identity issues because men never do. At the time, he basically just wore a bigger version of the athletic shorts and t-shirts our kids wore. Long gone were the suits and ties of his twenties and thirties now that he was mostly working from home and had nobody to impress but the cats. But at least he was supportive.

"You always look good to me," he said when he saw me standing in the closet near tears one day. "Maybe some tight stretch pants would be nice."

"I'm wearing tight stretch pants right now. Only they're not meant to be tight stretch pants. They're just regular pants that . . . I'm stretching."

And then he spent the next fifteen minutes reassuring me that I was still reasonably attractive for my age.

My hair was the easiest way to adjust my appearance to match how I was feeling on the inside, so I let it grow long, like it was in my early twenties when I couldn't afford haircuts. (I was so poor that I once volunteered to be a model at a beauticians' convention, and a psychotic stylist from Louisiana named Marc Anthony Franducci speed cut my hair on stage while the theme from *Mission Impossible* blasted. It was amazing, and I looked like Jon Bon Jovi when he finished.) It also wasn't hard to ditch my church bake sale twinset sweaters for form-fitting t-shirts that I bought from the stores in the mall that smell like patchouli. The t-shirts were printed with sayings like "SAVE MOTHER EARTH" and "RECYCLE THAT CAN, MAN," which felt a little juvenile but also gave me an easy way to express myself. Overall, it wasn't a great look, but I had at least attempted to find a new style, and I thought it was working for me—until once again, Mom Prom saw my nascent bubble of self-confidence and ran at me with a stick pin.

One hot Saturday morning, I found myself sitting next to three posh moms at Jack's Little League baseball game. The women were about the same age as me, but that's where the similarities ended.

All three of them were decked out in colorful maxi dresses and wedge sandals, with full makeup, blowouts, and even nail art. *Nail art.* I surreptitiously checked them out because I was sincerely confused by their appearance. I mean, it was 9 a.m. on a Saturday. We were at a ball field that didn't have real toilets. The only food available was dill pickle–flavored sunflower seeds sold at the snack stand by a preteen with a mustache. Did they have plans to go to a cotillion after the seventh inning, I wondered? Or to a Russian oligarch's yacht party? Or maybe our local baseball diamond now had a cocktail attire requirement that I didn't know about. At any rate, it was clear there'd been more grooming on their part for a kiddie sports event than there'd been on my part for my wedding. I kept that thought to myself, however, and just listened to them compliment each other while we all ignored the game being played in front of us.

"Gurlllllll, where DID you get those adorable platforms?"

"Aren't they to die for? Jeremy would get reallll upset if he knew how much they cost, but I just couldn't resist!"

"That's hilarious, gurlllllllll! You're so bad!"

"I know! Y'all, I'm so baddddddd. I have them in black too!"

As the kiss-ass session continued and the umpire called balls and strikes, my fragile new style confidence rapidly dwindled. A *Real Housewives of Austin* episode was happening in the bleachers, and the stars of the show were the three women toting thousand-dollar designer bags and, in my cat-hair-covered sweatshirt from the 75-percent-off clearance rack at Target, I was the random personal assistant who flinches every time the camera catches her scurrying around in the background. Completing my bleacher creature look that day was the hat on my head that featured a smiling skull and the words "Grateful Dead Tour Alumni." I was quite proud of that hat because I got it at a notorious Austin drug paraphernalia shop with the gift card I won in a downtown comedy club's sketch writing contest. But I didn't think that would impress the gurlllllllllls, so I kept my mouth shut and hoped they'd be hit in the head by a foul ball. Well, not hit hard. Just enough to mess up their blowouts a little.

What is it about being around fancy women like the Youth Sports Complex Glam Squad that can make you feel like shit? I thought I was long over worrying about fitting in with moms at school, long over comparing myself to them, and long over my fucking insecure high school emotions, for god's sake, but I felt like the ugly stepsister that day. But more than that: I was confused. Had I missed a few memos or something? Did our team even send out memos? Does anyone still send out memos? But was it now *de rigueur* to dress up for Little League? And if so, how did those moms have the skills and the time to look so put together this early, anyway? Fifteen minutes before the game I'd been scrambling to find my kid's uniform while yelling at him to flush the toilet and feed the cats, not glamming it up with false eyelashes and body glitter. The entire experience made me feel like I'd once again failed a test I didn't know I was taking. I'd later learn that one of those fancy moms is a former Miss Oklahoma, which I guess explains it a little more. At least she wasn't wearing her tiara that day.

Back to my Dillard's meltdown.

The reason I was on a shopping mission wasn't because I needed a sequined cocktail dress and elbow-length satin gloves for the Little League playoffs, but because I had to find something to wear onstage in the show I was producing. That's right, I'd recently entered the world of *showbiz*! Or at least the world of community theater. I'd had such a great experience at BlogHer 2009 when I read my essay to a big audience that I jumped at the chance to produce and direct a show in Austin called *Listen to Your Mother*. *LTYM* was a sensation that started in Madison, Wisconsin, by my good friend Ann Imig (who I met via our blogs), and it quickly expanded to over forty cities with local casts reading their original essays.

"The show is basically *The Vagina Monologues* but with fewer vaginas and more stories about motherhood, so I guess it'd be called *The Uterus Monologues* only not everyone in the show has a uterus, but they do all have monologues!" was my usual spiel. Now that I reread it, I kind of understand why I had a hard time getting sponsors. Maybe I should have pitched it as a MILF burlesque show.

I was passionate about my *Listen to Your Mother* event because I wanted to give other women and men the same life-changing opportunity I had when I shared my story in Chicago. I knew that I wasn't alone in hungering for connection and support, in wanting to have my voice heard, so I pushed myself out of my comfort zone to make it happen. Yes, the show was about motherhood, and yes, I didn't want to be typecast as a mother, but that was okay. It's not like I wanted to entirely shove that part of my life aside, anyway. Not that I could with my two little guys hanging around asking for snacks all the time. But more than that, stories about motherhood are all so individual and intense that it felt important to me to facilitate getting them out into the world. I still wasn't completely comfortable climbing on stage as the emcee of the show, but I soon discovered that I become *extremely* comfortable once I'm standing on the stage as the emcee of the show. My "off-the-cuff, freestyle riffing" while at the podium next to my co-emcee/producer/director Liz was quite something.

"Hi, I'm Liz and welcome to *Listen to Your Mother!*"

"Hi, I'm Wendi and thank you all for being here. How about those Longhorns, huh? Where you from, darlin'? Lubbock? I have an ex-husband in Lubbock. The things that man could do with a rope and a . . . OW, will you stop kicking me, Liz?"

Okay, it wasn't quite that bad, but I *was* repeatedly told to stick to the script and I did get a lot of bruises on my shin. The show was usually held around Mother's Day, so each year we'd read a hundred-plus submissions of motherhood essays, then hold auditions to get our cast of ten. It was a daunting process, as Liz was fond of saying. Especially during the tryouts when we couldn't make eye contact with each other or we'd lose it, like the time an auditioner hardcore rapped about her malfunctioning ovaries or when a sweet Southern women put a tin foil hat on her head and pretended to talk to her grandmother in heaven.

"Meemaw, I know y'all want the best for me, and I hope you're making friends with the angels. Do they have harps? Or those little mouth harmonicas like the big guy from Blues Traveler?"

It was fun and weird and exciting to do a show, but the best part about *LTYM* was how it introduced me to a community of dynamic writers, most of whom I now consider good friends. Some even went on to have their writing produced in plays and published in places like *The Paris Review*. And the even better part was that most of these writers lived in Austin, so I was able to see them more than once a year at a conference. My world was expanding yet again because I tried something challenging and a little bit scary. I was proud of *LTYM* because it felt important and worthy, so of course my stage outfit had to be amazing.

That day at Dillard's, I stood in the middle of the sprawling second floor, batting away the perfume sprayers, listening to the piped-in Celine Dion music, and glanced at the clothing departments surrounding me: Juniors, Plus Sizes, Petites, Workout Wear, Club Kids, Pottery-Making Therapists, Grandmas on a Cruise, Trophy Wives, Slutty Lumberjacks, etc. I then looked harder at each section and realized with a sinking feeling that I didn't know where I belonged. I wandered into Juniors, and a saleswoman asked me if I was looking for my daughter. Too old. I wandered into the sensible slacks and blouses department, and a saleswoman asked me if I was looking for my mother. Too young. I was glared at by a short woman in Petites. Too tall. And the five-hundred-dollar suit section wasn't a fit, either. Too poor. I was Suburban Goldilocks yet again. Where was the "just right" section? Where was the "Middle" section? Where was the section with clothes that'd show how youthful I felt on the inside, even though I didn't necessarily look like that on the outside? Fuck porridge, I just wanted a dress that didn't make me look like an out-of-touch lady troll.

Feeling shunned in every department, I slunk into the demilitarized zone between the Reba section and the Ralph Lauren section, and the tears finally started. "Life would be a lot easier if I just loved clothing with a kicky country flair," I thought miserably while I watched a woman my age gleefully grab a Reba shirt covered in rhinestones and images of horses running on a prairie. "Look at how happy she is with her rodeo-inspired wear. Why can't I figure this out? Why won't someone just shove some clothes at me and say, 'Wear these, dummy.' I need a fairy god . . . oddd . . . mooother." Then a nearby salesclerk asked if I had just wiped my nose on an eighty-dollar patchwork sweater, and I had to run away before she found out the answer was yes.

A few weeks later, I somehow got my wish when my fairy godmother actually showed up—via Nextdoor.com, not an enchanted pumpkin, but who cares. A woman named Jennifer in my neighborhood had started a wardrobe consulting business and offered her services to me for free as a trial run. I assume because she'd seen me hunched in the corner of the bleachers at the Little League cotillion. It didn't matter how she found me because I was thrilled.

The first thing I did was fill out a questionnaire detailing what I like to wear (I'm not sure), what my lifestyle is like (I'm not sure), and list my fashion inspiration (1970s Manilow and/or Blair on *The Facts of Life*?) Then one weekday morning, she and her partner showed up at my house, and we went through my closet and drawers and put everything that "wasn't working" in a pile. There was a lot that wasn't working. Like the eighteen pairs of khaki pants that I didn't even know I owned. At one point Chris saw the pile and asked, "What is that? Why so many tan pants? Were you hoping to be hired by Target?"

It was somewhat embarrassing and uncomfortable to have strangers dig through my wardrobe, but it was also completely worth it. A few hours after starting, the wardrobe consultants showed me the clothes that I needed get rid of (a lot) and the pieces that were okay to keep (not a lot). They then magically put together new outfits for me with clothes I already owned. Combinations I would have never figured out on my own. A white jacket goes with that? Really? And as if that wasn't enough, we then hopped in the car and went to Nordstrom so I could buy a few new pieces. Jennifer reinforced to me the "pay more for an article of clothing you'll wear a lot" theory. Much smarter than my "OMG it's a purple glitter Snoopy XXXL tank top and it's only two-ninety-nine on sale so I should buy ten of them" strategy that I'd been riding for years.

"You need to stop letting your style be dictated by what's on the 75-percent-off rack," she told me while I bagged up my cast-offs for Goodwill. "That goes for the 50-percent-off rack too. If it's something that nobody else wanted to buy, don't touch it."

And that was that. In just a few hours, I had an edited closet, photos of my outfits, a shopping list, and links to store websites so I could easily buy what I needed. It was all tailored just for me and my lifestyle and my personality, not for my age. Imagine that. But by putting my trust in Jennifer and her partner to do something I couldn't do myself, which was see me with fresh eyes and recognize what was no longer working and where I was headed, I kind of found my style. And with that came an increase in confidence that is often hard to come by in middle age when it's easy to think the style ship has sailed. But the best part of all? They helped me find the perfect dress to wear for that year's *Listen to Your Mother* show.

Needless to say, it wasn't from Dillard's.

THINGS THAT MAKE A WOMAN LOOK COOL IF SHE'S UNDER 40 AND A BIT NUTS IF SHE'S OVER 40

There's no age limit on what women may choose to wear, but here's a secret: there actually are a few things you just can't pull off after a certain age. Not without looking like you're ready to be checked into the Trembling Acres Rest Home for Active Wingnuts, anyway. For that reason, I've written up the following list of what you probably shouldn't wear or do if you're forty-plus. Of course, if you still decide to try any of these things, I really can't stop you. You're a grown-ass woman.

Pigtails
Under forty: Cute cheerleader
Over forty: White zinfandel day drinker

Traveling with an emotional support cat
Under forty: Adorable hipster animal rescuer
Over forty: Creepy animal hoarder

Playing ukulele on a park bench
Under forty: Whimsical
Over forty: Homicidal

Wearing sunglasses indoors
Under forty: Mysterious and glamorous
Over forty: You have glaucoma or you're Anna Wintour or both

A t-shirt that says "I LOVE CUTE BOYS"
Under forty: Ooh, she's a cougar!
Over forty: Ewww, she's a cougar.

Buying condoms in bulk at Costco
Under forty: That woman is sexually adventurous!
Over forty: That woman is running a brothel in her minivan!

A hat that's slightly askew
Under forty: You're into streetwear
Over forty: You're into mixing medications

Showing sideboob
Under forty: Leaves them wanting more
Over forty: Leaves them wanting no more, please god, no more

An all-denim outfit
Under forty: On the cutting edge of fashion
Over forty: On a work release program

Twerking
Under forty: That woman has MOVES
Over forty: Does that woman have a MedicAlert bracelet?

Low-rise jeans
Under forty: It's so sexy to show off a little skin
Over forty: Is that a faded Def Leppard tramp stamp on Brenda?

A floral crown/outfit made entirely of scarves:
Under forty: I'm on my way to Coachella!
Over forty: I'm on my way to my fortune teller job!

'80s legwarmers

Under forty: You're wearing them because they're back in style

Over forty: You're wearing them because you didn't know they ever went out of style

Roller-skating to work

Under forty: "I'm athletic and environmentally friendly!"

Over forty: "I lost my license for running a brothel in my minivan"

How to Throw Yourself a Middle-Age-Reveal Party

Are you confused by your stage of life? Feel young and vibrant, and yet a day-spa worker recently called your skin "crêpey"? It'd be great to finally have confirmation that you're no longer a vital part of society—but how? Throw yourself a middle-age-reveal party!
Here's a step-by-step guide:

Decide on a Theme
Most middle-age-reveal parties share a simple theme: gray. Think gray cocktails, gray plastic cups, gray napkins, and gray party games, such as Pin the Sad Gray Tail on the Sad Gray Donkey Who Looks Ridiculous in Floral Prints. If gray's not your color, simply build a theme around something that you love to do—for example, eating couch snacks while watching *Murder, She Wrote.*

Set the Date
Send invitations to your reveal four to six weeks in advance. Cute invitations can be found online through Etsy and Paperless Post. If you're tempted to buy them at a stationery store in the mall, the party is no longer necessary: it's already been revealed that you're an old bitch.

Plan a Welcome Game for Guests
Kick things off by asking guests to guess your age! If they guess lower than it actually is, hand them a prize like a yummy fruit skewer. If they guess higher, hand them a prize like your middle finger and a now-strained relationship.

Pick a Dramatic Way to Reveal Whether You're Middle-Aged

The fun of this event is keeping everyone—including yourself!—in suspense until it's time for the grand reveal (much like your period when it disappears for two months and then rages on back during your anniversary beach vacation). Some awesome ways to find out if you're middle-aged at a party—rather than at a wine bar, when a graduate student with a man bun calls you "ma'am"—include:

• Knee Test: Squat down to grab something out of a low cabinet, like a colander or a cake pan. If you can stand back up without assistance, you are not in middle age. But if you slowly tip over onto your side while hissing "Fuckkkkkk this life," you are!

• The Scroll: While guests watch, log on to a website that requires you to enter the year in which you were born via a drop-down menu. Now see how long it takes you to scroll down far enough to find that year. Two minutes? Three? Do you see 1929 at the bottom of the list? Then—ding-ding-ding! Hello, oldie.

• Menu Reading: Have a party guest hand you a restaurant menu. Without using glasses, a flashlight app, candlelight, or a child's help, try to read at least three items. If you make it to the salads section without throwing the menu across the room and shrieking, "What the hell! Is this a restaurant for mice?"—congratulations! You are still considered attractive by some.

• Piñata Time!: Hang up a man-shaped piñata, then grab a bat. If you just gently knock the piñata around a few times, you are not in middle age. But if you whack the shit out of that crêpe-paper motherfucker like it just voted to take away your reproductive rights, all while screaming, "DEATH TO THE PATRIARCHY! EAT PAIN, DIPSHIT!," your AARP card is already in the mail. You'll also need some Motrin for your sore biceps.

• Box o' Fucks: Two boxes labeled "fucks" are placed on a table. You must choose one, and only one, to open. If the box you choose is full of fucks, you are not in middle age. Go buy a crop top on Instagram, kid. But if you open a box and there are no fucks inside—if there are no fucks left to give and you couldn't find a fuck even if you used a fucking fuck detector—guess what? You're middle-aged, baby. And that means the party's now over. Send your guests home. It's time to cry-eat and watch *Murder, She Wrote*.

CHAPTER SIX

I'M WEARING FURY NOW

My political awakening happened on a Friday afternoon. It was July 26, 2013, and I was home doing important work on my laptop, which means reading @BarryManilow's Twitter, when I noticed a lot of local chatter about something happening at the Texas Capitol in downtown Austin. The buzz was about a state senator named Wendy Davis from Ft. Worth who'd begun what would become a thirteen-hour filibuster concerning the sweeping abortion restrictions the Texas Legislature, a group of mostly old white men, was about to pass. I followed the news for a while, then tried to go about my day. But I kept going back to my computer to read the live tweets and to watch the grainy video feed of the proceedings. It was captivating and unlike anything I'd ever seen before. Certainly not in Texas. Finally, around dinnertime, I grabbed my purse and my phone and told Chris and the boys that I was headed to the Capitol.

"I don't know if I'll get in or what exactly is going on, and I don't think anyone I know is there, but I just need to be in that room," I said to them with a bit of challenge in my eyes.

"Go, Wendi," Chris said without hesitation. "And also, go Wendy."

I love the moments when I know I married right.

I arrived at the imposing pink granite Capitol building on Congress Avenue that hot July evening, unsure of what I'd find. The first thing I noticed was that women were everywhere. This would become a common sight at the Capitol over the next few years, but I didn't know that yet. Nor did I know that I was about to launch into the pissed-off-raging-feminist-political-junkie-activist phase of my midlife years. I looked around the building and the grounds and saw women on the grand lawn, women next to the statues of (supposedly) heroic men, and women lined up to get into the building. They talked with each other in hushed, excited voices and carried themselves with purpose. Some were with organized groups, but most had come alone, like me. Many would later become my good friends and protest-mates, but I didn't know that yet, either.

I passed through security, noting that the woman in front of me was savvy and experienced enough to bring a plastic coat hanger that wouldn't set off the metal detector, and then entered the sausage factory that is the Texas Capitol. I paused next to the marble statue of Stephen F. Austin that's near the painting of Davy Crockett and adjacent to the beautiful rotunda lined with portrait after portrait of gentleman governors, but none of their blank male gazes intimidated me. That night the energy inside the Hall of Big Important Men felt feminine. Electric. Like something long asleep was finally waking up, ready to stop taking shit and start kicking ass. I know that sounds like a lame Goddess Power t-shirt you'd buy on Instagram at 2 a.m., but I don't care because it's true.

I followed the crowd up the grand staircase to the second floor and joined the long line of people waiting get into the Senate chamber gallery to watch Senator Davis's filibuster. The queue was almost fifty deep at each entrance, with women of all ages and backgrounds and ethnicities, and a few men, eager to witness and support Wendy. Intimidating Texas Rangers in stiff Stetsons and brown, pressed uniforms, guns and tasers strapped to their belts, stood guard at the doors. On previous visits, I found them to be serious, but also ready with a quick smile, tip of the hat, and polite, "Good afternoon, ma'am." Not this time. They'd let someone into the room only when someone left the room. One out, one in. It was like a nightclub but without the velvet ropes, VIP list, and hedge funders named Geoff hoovering coke in the bathroom.

This year's hottest club is FILIBUSTER. It has everything. Cowboy hats, misogynists, protest signs, white men with no working knowledge of female anatomy passing legislation about female anatomy, and Old Lady Roundup, that favorite Republican sport where they rustle up elderly Southern women and throw them out on their asses.

Those stoic Texas Rangers did indeed usher a few of the more "unruly" women out of the gallery later in the evening's proceedings. Unruly is in quotes because those women weren't brandishing weapons and threatening people, like the many gun nut protestors I've seen on the Capitol steps do. The "troublemaking women" just got a little too loud and passionate. One of the biggest loudmouths was my friend Ruth Pennebaker, who never lets me forget her legendary rabble rousing whenever I bring up the filibuster.

"I'm so proud of us for being there that night to witness history being made."

"Yes, but only one of us was a seventy-year-old woman dragged out of the room by the asshole Texas Rangers, and it wasn't you, darlin'."

Ruth recently told me that's going on her tombstone.

After waiting for about an hour, I finally walked into the Senate chambers. I'd been there a few times before on tours and for the Texas Book Festival where I'd watched interviews with famous authors, but this wasn't the tote-bag-carrying literary crowd raptly listening to Tom Perrotta talking about the suburban, sexual undertones in his latest novel about unhappy white people, this was completely different.

I sat in the first gallery seat I found open, an uncomfortable wooden one with no leg room, probably by design, and focused on Wendy. She held court on the green-carpeted Senate floor, about thirty feet below. Surrounding me were energized, focused, passionate women, many wearing Planned Parenthood t-shirts and many holding protest signs that said things like, "My Body, My Choice" and "Women's Rights Are Human Rights." The signs were fairly tame back then, unlike now when posterboards are covered in f-bombs and graphic suggestions of what men should do to their private parts. As with every pro-choice event, a few women waved coat hangers to symbolize the danger of illegal abortions. I smiled at the white-haired lady next to me who held a sign that read, "I Can't Believe I'm Still Protesting This Sh*t," not realizing how often I'd see other older women waving around that same sentiment over the next few years. Also not realizing how much I'd relate to it when the GOP's attacks on women's rights, rights I'd taken for granted most of my life, only became more harsh, prohibitive, and cruel.

Those of us in the gallery that night watched Senator Wendy Davis more than hold her own against the majority of the legislature. Some lawmakers looked like it was business as usual, some looked like it was a waste of their time, and a few actually seemed pained to be at the mercy of her filibuster. Imagine how awful it must have felt to them to have a woman take away their freedom to go home to their beds. The *nerve*. Not surprisingly, the men's tactic was to constantly interrupt her. "Uh, Ms. Davis, are you aware that blah blah blah I have a penis blah blah blabbity blah and it's a big one blooooopity bloop." But their jabbering and their lame points of order didn't deter her. She talked and kept talking and ignored the mansplainers with aplomb.

To ensure that she'd be comfortable standing for thirteen-plus hours—in a filibuster you're not allowed to sit, leave the room, or stop talking—Wendy wore her soon-to-be iconic pink running shoes and a long white cardigan. She was a bright, hopeful spot in the sea of dark suits. But it was her calm, measured Texas drawl, clearly stating the facts and statistics about women's healthcare, about the dangers the laws would cause, that was the real focus. She was prepared and in control and a hero to many that night. She was the woman we hung our hopes on and the one who ignited the political force that is pissed-off Texas women.

Before long, I started to live tweet what Wendy was saying. I confess that I'm somewhat of a wannabe cub reporter, albeit one who is sometimes grammar-challenged and more prone to making jokes than sticking to dry facts. I also hadn't studied up in advance, so I didn't entirely understand the proposed bill or the protocol of the legislature. Still, I tried to share what I was hearing to the best of my ability. The first replies, likes, and retweets that pinged back to me were from the followers and friends who usually chime in, but soon my tweets were being liked and shared by people all over the country. Then all over the world. The #StandWithWendy hashtag began to trend on Twitter as more followers and the real journalists in the room amplified it from their phones. The filibuster captivated thousands that night, maybe millions, much like it captivated me earlier in the day. The Republicans in the Texas legislature were being called out on their sexist, controlling bullshit for the first time in a long time—and on a worldwide stage to boot. It felt good to know that we weren't alone. That we had so many allies also bearing witness to Wendy's fight.

After three or four hours in my hard gallery seat, I reluctantly gave up my spot due to a dead phone battery and a full bladder—no pee breaks allowed—and I left the Capitol to go home. I've wished many times since that I'd stayed because later that night, Cecile Richards, then-president of Planned Parenthood, stood under the Texas dome next to the official portrait of her revered, badass mother, Governor Ann Richards, one of only two female governors hanging on the wall, and gave an impassioned speech about our fight for reproductive rights. The hundreds of Texas women and men lining the four stories of the limestone rotunda chanted and cheered and sang the University of Texas's spirit song, "The Eyes of Texas." If you haven't seen the video, find it and watch. It still gives me chills. My friend Martha was there and said, "It felt like the walls of the Texas Capitol were shaking with the power of our protest."

A day or so later, that momentum continued via a big reproductive freedom rally outside the Capitol, with speeches by Democratic lawmakers and city leaders and music performances by locals like Natalie Maines of The Chicks. Thousands of women gathered to chant and to march and to let the Republicans know that what they were doing was wrong and unfair and we were no longer going to take it quietly. Their secret backroom deals weren't going to be so easy anymore—we were paying attention. I stood in the hot sun with my recently rousted friend Ruth and her daughter that day in our matching orange t-shirts that said, "Wendy Is My Mob Boss," inspired by one of the GOPers calling the female protestors "an unruly mob" (yes, Ruth, *you* were the unruliest) and knew that my life was changed.

I certainly hadn't planned to become a middle-aged activist. Or Midctivist. Oldtivist? Okay those don't quite work. But in my late-forties, I was busy with my kids and my writing and with planning family vacations to places like Universal Studios, where the worst thing that can happen to a woman's body is getting jostled so much that you leak pee on the Minion Adventure ride. Not that that's ever happened to me, of course. I do my kegels.

But like Gloria Steinem said, "The truth will set you free, but first it will piss you off." After that night at the Capitol, I started to see sexism and inequality everywhere and it made me furious. I thought critically for the first time about my experience in Hollywood and the opportunities I didn't get because I was a woman. I'd always thought there was something I was doing wrong. That I wasn't smart enough, or educated enough, or connected enough, or big-boobed enough. But in those places of male hierarchy, the deck was stacked against me the whole time, even as a white woman of privilege. For women of color and LGBTQIA+ people, the deck is stacked a million times higher. Add in pay gaps, maternal mortality, rapists that go unpunished, medical gaslighting, missing and murdered Indigenous women, attacks on democracy, racist voting restrictions, just to name a few travesties, and the world looks like a pretty bleak place.

It soon became difficult to not burn with rage 24/7. Sometimes my anger would come out at inopportune times too, like on our family trip to Disneyland when I sat with Sam and Jack and watched the Snow White play. After one of the actors leaned over the immobile woman who'd fallen into a coma due to eating a poison apple and said, "I'm so sad she's dead, she was so beautiful," I immediately turned to the boys and snarled, "AND SHE IS ALSO SMART AND KIND AND ACCOMPLISHED AND MUCH MORE THAN HER LOOKS! THAT PRINCE IS SEXIST! AND SO ARE THE DWARVES! ALL SEVEN OF THEM! DO YOU UNDERSTAND, BOYS?" Seriously, get your gender stereotyping shit together, Dopey.

At long last, I was finally using my voice without caring who heard it. Or caring if using it meant someone wouldn't like me because of my thoughts and beliefs. That comes naturally with age, but it coincided with what was starting to happen politically too. It was a big step for a person who never liked to speak up publicly lest the moms at school get upset. I now found myself at school pickup, listening to a horribly stuck-up woman who I'd put up with for years saying something rude about immigrants, but instead of ignoring her like usual, I slid up to her, got next to her ear and hissed, "Shut the hell up and read a newspaper, Jessica." I felt like Tony friggin' Soprano.

Then I grabbed the boys and walked away on shaky legs hoping she wouldn't throw a playground rock at my head.

It was scary to finally start speaking up about politics and social issues, but it also felt like I was finally being honest about who I really was. Even a year earlier, I kept my political thoughts secret from people in my day-to-day life despite my rage-inspired love of political satire. I kept quiet even as I started cowriting a wildly popular political parody Twitter account that went viral. In 2012, after Paul Ryan announced he was Mitt Romney's running mate, my blogging friend Karen came up with the idea of merging him with Ryan Gosling's "Hey girl" meme and thus @PaulRyanGosling was birthed in a loud burst of satire and snark. Karen and I, and our friends Mariana, Kelcey, and Kristine, started writing and posting gems like this:

@PaulRyanGosling Hey girl, I hope you're middle-class because I can't wait to screw you.

@PaulRyanGosling Hey girl, I'm going to defund Planned Parenthood. Unplanned Parenthood is just so much more whimsical.

@PaulRyanGosling Hey girl, good news! Early voting starts in Ohio today, so you don't have to wait until November to give away your reproductive rights!

Not exactly Shakespeare, but they were definitely funny. Importantly, we didn't let anyone know that we were the writers behind the account, which felt both good and bad. Good, because we could say whatever we wanted and make sharp, entertaining, political comments that were taken seriously. But also bad because I wanted people to know that I was a part of it. At its peak, the account had almost a hundred-thousand followers, and our tweets were shown on TV news programs, including *The Rachel Maddow Show* and *Today*, and reposted in various newspapers and magazines around the world. Once, we were even shut down by Twitter for forty-eight hours after the Paul Ryan campaign complained that we were falsely impersonating him. Yep. They faxed a copy of his driver's license to Twitter HQ to prove he was who he said he was, and we then had to change our Twitter bio to say, "PARODY. Role-playing. Not affiliated with Speaker Paul Ryan or actor Ryan Gosling. Obviously." I still believe that my group of politically engaged friends were as smart and as funny as any writers for *The Daily Show* or *SNL* at the time.

But then sexism entered the chat like it always does. A woman from *New York Magazine* asked to write a profile about us. We agreed to be interviewed and have our real identities finally disclosed, but I specifically said to her, "Don't mention that we're moms. That's not what's important. We're five smart satirists that care about the election. The fact that we're mothers is beside the point." The story came out with the headline, "Meet the Mom Bloggers Behind @PaulRyanGosling" and all we could say was, "Hey girl, what the fuck."

The female rage and activism that erupted in Texas in 2013 hit a national scale a couple of years later when a malevolent orange moron with tiny hands inexplicably became president. The shock and despair that a racist, sexist cheater, the one who famously said "grab 'em by the pussy," won the highest office in America galvanized women across the country, and the Women's March of 2017 was a breathtaking display of collective power and anger. And the majority of people in those crowds? *Middle-aged* women. This fact isn't often highlighted when discussing the story of the Women's March, or if it is, it's in a condescending manner. "These Minivan Drivers Have Had It Up to Here!" "Menopausers Take to the Streets!" But it was obvious to anyone who looked around the crowd that most of the women protesting owned a Walkman at one point. Most could easily name ten bands from the '80s. Some of them may have been *in* ten bands from the '80s, like my friend Kathy Valentine of The Go-Go's, who I've stood shoulder-to-shoulder with at many rallies in Austin.

Gen-X women are one of the most politically active demographic groups right now. Is this because women forty-plus are just pissed off in general? Is it because by this time in our lives, we're tired of decade after decade of taking everyone's shit? I'm sure that's part of it. But it's also because middle-aged women have realized that we can use the skills and influence and experiences we've spent our lives honing to leave a better world for younger generations. We know that things aren't *supposed* to be like this. It was pure luck that I was born into a body and a place that meant I didn't have to struggle for most basic human and civil rights. What finally lit a fire under me was when the political became personal and the hard-won women's reproductive rights I took for granted were under attack, but that was just the start. Now, I'm all in.

There was one upside to the orange moron's term: it spurred an unprecedented number of women to run for office. One of them was a woman I'd inexplicably become friends with after a chance meeting, a Texan named MJ Hegar. She's a mom, wife, MBA, and decorated war hero who was awarded the Purple Heart for fighting off the Taliban in Afghanistan in her helicopter and being shot down. Yep, you could say I leveled-up in the friend arena from those old Drunko days. MJ ran for Congress in 2018 against an old, white Texas Tea Partier who'd

also never before been called on his bullshit, and despite not knowing
what I was doing, I eagerly jumped in to help get her movement off
the ground. At the age of fifty, I was beyond proud to work on my very
first political campaign.

MJ didn't win that race, but she inspired people around the world.
That's crucial because over the past few years, the patriarchy, which is
a word I admit that I probably didn't even know in the '80s and '90s,
has been working overtime to turn back equality, human rights, and
environmental progress. The list of issues to get politically active about
is pretty much endless, and there's no end in sight. And if you don't do
anything because you're okay with the status quo? Don't let the door
hit your ass on the way out, chump. I said a permanent goodbye to a
lot of former friends and acquaintances, both on social media and in
real life, after the 2016 presidential election in a move that I called
THE GREAT UNFRIENDING. It needed to happen and resulted
in the women I'm closest with now being women who aren't taking
this shit lying down.

I went to an event a couple years ago in downtown Austin that
some friends had organized for Constitution Day. (Another thing
I admit that I probably didn't know about in the '80s and '90s. Did
you know there's a day for celebrating the Constitution?) As I looked
around the room, I saw Carrie, the maker of the "Come and Take It"
bumper stickers that she passed out at the Wendy Davis rally, who
had also started a group that massively increased voter turnout in
South Austin, and Anne, who inspired me and many others to block
walk and organize for our candidates. I looked at Susanne, who was so
outraged by bigots targeting sex education in the Austin public school
system that she organized a group that fights to get an inclusive
curriculum passed, and at my friends Meredith, Laura, and Jill, who
had just returned from taking supplies to an immigrant center on the

Texas border. The room was filled with passionate, outspoken women who chose to spend their afternoon writing postcards, learning about voter registration, and discussing what we needed to work on next to make Texas a livable state for everyone. It cemented my belief that the future may or may not be female, but my present is middle-aged women fighting to make sure that whatever future we have is one that's fair and equal for all.

The Texas Republicans managed to pass that restrictive bill in 2013, and there's been a lot of back and forth on similar—and worse— legislation since then. But even though they "won," they also lost. Because their actions on that hot night in 2013 spurred thousands of Texas women to finally wake up and get angry. I know I sure as hell did.

PROTEST SIGNS I'D RATHER BE HOLDING

Think Globally, Wax Locally

If You're Not Outraged, You're Not Paying Attention to Nextdoor

I Still Can't Believe I Have to Protest This Shit When
My Back Hurts So Bad

Remember the Alamo, Forget Where I Put My Keys

This Sign Sponsored by AARP

Pill, Baby, Pill

Yes, We Can! If We Don't Have to Drive After Dark

We're Here! We're Queer! We Need to Be in Bed by 9 p.m.!

Make Love, Not War, but Not Tonight Because I'm Sweaty

Fraternité, Égalité, Pumpkin Spice Latte

Power to the People Who Didn't Read the Book Before Book Club

Eat the Rich (They're only 44 Weight Watchers Points!)

What Do We Want? COOLING SHEETS
When Do We Want Them? EVERY FUCKING NIGHT

Better Dead Than Miss Clairol Red

Hell No, We Won't Go to Costco on a Saturday

My Body, My Choice to Have a Perimenopause Mustache

A Chicken in Every Pot and a Forgotten Cup of Coffee
in Every Microwave

Give Me Lipitor or Give Me Death

Come and Take It Because I'm Downsizing

Lips That Touch Liquor Are Probably Mine

I Can't See the Menu without a Flashlight, But I Can See Your Bias

Make My Ass Great Again

CHAPTER SEVEN

NO ONE CARES WHAT I'M WEARING NOW

I took customer service for granted when I was fertile. Breezing up to the counter, I'd be immediately addressed by the barista, maybe even engaged in small talk about the weather or what I had goin' on for the weekend, then the employee would smile, look me in the eye and hand me a nonfat latte with my forever coffee shop name of WINDY scrawled on the cup, and I'd go on my merry way. It was nice.

Once I hit my late forties, my coffee shop experience became more like a basic cable ad for putting mom in a home. "Oh, sorry I didn't see you there, ma'am. Did you want something? I SAID DO YOU WANT SOMETHING? ARE YOU LOST? DO YOU NEED ME TO CALL IN A SILVER ALERT?" No, dum-dum, I don't want something. I just vaporized into this Starbucks from an air vent so I could silently watch you flirt with a man bun wearing Lululemon joggers and hemp socks, and now I shall return to the middle-aged ether in a poof of cat dander to go spend my day sipping tea made from moth wings while I read my copy of 1986's *People*'s Sexiest Men Alive issue with Mark Harmon on the cover. Fare thee well, child. Fare thee *welllllllll.*

For fuck's sake.

Middle-aged women often complain that they feel invisible, but that's only because we are. Slowly, then all of a sudden, I realized that I now blend into the background. Once my face had a few more wrinkles and my hair turned a little grayer, I became undetectable to the human eye. Men no longer notice me, younger women no longer notice me, and store clerks only glance my way when I accidentally knock a jar of pickles off the shelf, then blame it on the nearest baby. This erasure eventually happens to all of us. The only people that actually pay attention to forty-plus women in public are other forty-plus women, and then we just shoot each other a quick glance to see if they're someone mean from the PTO that we want to avoid. Ninety percent of the cardio I get is from sprinting away from some Sass-Mouth Sally at the grocery store.

For the record, I and other Gen-X women aren't actually invisible. We haven't actually disappeared. The Aqua Net and Love's Baby Soft fumes we huffed in the '80s didn't cause some sort of molecular change that now allows us to walk through walls like Casper the Friendly Ghost, even though that would be amazing and save me a ton of cash on movie tickets. Our bodies can still be seen. It's just that now nobody wants to see them.

I'm not upset about this because there's not much point. It's just nature's way. According to something I read on the back of a box of perimenopausal tea at Whole Foods, then quickly shoved back on the shelf because it cost twenty-four dollars, the reason we oldies are ignored is biological. It's simply how humans protect the species. We're (most likely) no longer able to reproduce and therefore no longer sexually viable and therefore disgusting skags who shouldn't even be allowed to post selfies on Instagram without a trigger warning. ("Caution: Unfiltered Fifty-Year-Old Lady Face Ahead.") Once our main bodily purpose in life is over, we're no longer desired. We no longer get attention because our wombs are like one of those abandoned suburban malls where the possums have taken over. It's Science with a capital S. And I guess I'm usually okay with that until the moment I try to order a gin and tonic on a busy Friday night and can't catch the bartender's eye because my eggs are all dried up. I don't want to have your stupid baby, Jaxson, but I still get *thirsty*, motherfucker.

The women who are still of fertile age, the viable egg crew, are the opposite of invisible. They're seen strutting all over town in their floppy Instagram hats and firm skin and barely used reproductive systems. They're turning heads, taking names, and pulling all focus. And I get it. I mean, why would a horny dude check me out when he could instead check out some hottie who didn't incorporate Sea Breeze and Gee, Your Hair Smells Terrific into her teenage beauty regimen? The human urge to propagate is strong, and I'm obviously not going to continue someone's DNA at this point. Not unless I sign up for a random clinical trial and end up trapped in the sheep cloning laboratory at Texas A&M, anyway. But even though I understand all of that on an intellectual level, I admit that feeling invisible can be painful. Sometimes literally.

A few years back, I was at a furniture warehouse in East Austin to pick up our new solid wood coffee table, and I almost lost a body part in the process. Two of the loading dock bros were helping me lift the table into the back of my SUV that day, and it wasn't going well. After a few grunts and muscle flexes, we almost had that heavy beast off the ground, but then a twenty-something woman with a KardashaJenner booty passed us on her way to the lighting section. Boom. Biology had arrived. Their penises told their brains, "STOP WHAT YOU'RE DOING WITH THE GROSS OLDIE! YOUR MASTER DNA COMMANDS YOU!", and they both immediately became so entranced by this woman's obvious and bangable fertility that they dropped the table right onto my foot. Seconds passed without anyone remembering that I existed as a human being on this planet until I began to scream like a European soccer player after a swift kick to the nuts.

"OWWWWW. HELPPPPPPPPP. OWWWWW."

"Huh? Oh, sorry, ma'am," one of the jabronies said, not taking his gaze off the KardashaJenner who was slowly bending over to retrieve her phone from her purse.

"OWWWWW. HELPPPPPPPPP. OWWWWW."

"You need something, ma'am?" the other jabroni asked, also not taking his gaze off the KardashaJenner who had now moved on to a slow-motion lip-gloss application session.

"TAKE. THE. FUCKING. TABLE. OFF. MY. FUCKING. FOOT."

I now understand why some stores have special shopping hours for Seniors. It's so someone will notice if a shelving unit collapses and pins them to the ground.

It's not lost on me how ironic it is that I finally found my wardrobe style right before I became invisible. Now nobody notices if I'm even wearing clothes. I could probably strut around an Alabama demolition derby in an "I Miss Obama" t-shirt and a pink pussy hat and come out unscathed. My friend Emily says that once you're over forty, men look at you and think "vague woman shape, not screwable, pass." But it's not just men. Most people see a middle-aged female headed their way, maybe wearing sensible shoes because her back hurts, a weird hat because she doesn't want any more sun damage, and an ill-fitting promotional t-shirt from a credit union that she found in a dark corner of the laundry room, and immediately dismiss her. Immediately assume she has nothing to contribute to the conversation. (I know not every woman my age dresses like what I described, but I just looked at my reflection in my laptop screen and guess what.) It wasn't true in my foot injury situation, but is this midlife erasure why some women go fucking nuts in public? Is it the reason some of them end up on YouTube screaming at the top of their lungs and causing a scene? Just so people finally pay some attention to them?

No. It's because they're racists.

I was sort of okay with becoming invisible in public when it first started. I don't like getting that much attention, anyway. The phrase, "Let's go around the room and introduce ourselves!" sends me straight into a bout of irritable bowel syndrome. But what really stung was when I began to disappear in my own house. By the time I was in my late forties, Sam and Jack were in middle school and high school and didn't need me as much. Or at all. The days of cutting grapes in half and being awakened at 6 a.m. by a chubby, sticky toddler hand to the face were long gone. They now slept until noon, and I had to wake them up by snarkily asking if they planned to sleep through the best part of the day like my mom used to ask me. She still does if I sleep past 8 a.m. (For the record, I *always* plan on sleeping through the best part of the day.) But after ten-plus years on the job, I was no longer on full-time mom patrol. Or even part-time. I was more like a seasonal employee who secretly drinks in the break room and gets fired for stealing a few laptops from the warehouse. The boys weren't stuck to my side because they were busy with school and friends and sports and video games and rolling their eyes at most of the family activities Chris and I tried to get them to enjoy.

"Sam, could you at least pretend you like being at the zoo?"

"Fine, but it's not like any of the animals in cages are having a good time, either."

This independence (and insouciance) is a parent's goal, of course. No mother wants to tuck their fifteen-year-old into bed every night, and not just because he now smells like a wheel of Brie that's been left on the sidewalk. But the teenage years are a hell of a change for parents because you're no longer the center of your kid's universe. You've been downgraded from the sun to a rando quasar that appears every now and then to nag them about unloading the dishwasher. The hardest part about these years for me wasn't that the boys were wild or disobedient teens because they weren't at all. They were just elsewhere, both mentally and physically. For years I'd yelled, "I just want some time to myself!" and then wham! I suddenly had it. Maybe too much of it. The dynamic had shifted, and now I was the one popping into their rooms to ask if they wanted to watch a show with me. Or go to the park with me. Or anything, really.

One night Chris found me in my closet holding a glass of wine in one hand and a cat in the other, quietly crying. He nicely overlooked that I seemed to be Ack! cosplaying a *Cathy* cartoon and gave me a concerned hug.

"What's going on?" he asked. "Did something happen?"

"Not really. It's just that I saw the gingerbread houses the boys and I used to make every year at the store today, and some mom was there with her little guy, and he was super excited and cute, and that's how they used to be," I choked out. "But they're big and they don't need me anymore. They'd hate making a gingerbread house with me now."

"Aw, they love you, you know that," he said. "And you should go back and buy the gingerbread house. They'll do it with you. *I'll make sure of that.*"

He meant well, as he always does, but nobody wants their kids to hang out with them because their dad went threat level midnight on their ass. It's just not the same. I wanted them to *want* to be with me like they did when they were little. Chris maybe didn't understand this because he didn't feel the absence of the boys' attention nearly as much as I did. For one, he'd never been home all day every day because he mostly worked outside of the house when they were small. But he'd also recently made a big midlife career transition that kept him busy and engaged. From the time we first met over that keg in Reno, he'd worked in public relations and marketing for various high-tech companies. Don't ask me what he did in that capacity because my mind usually drifted to thoughts about cake or "Was George Michael ever really happy?" whenever he talked about work. But his dream was always to teach at a college level, so in his late forties he took a job teaching a night class at an HBCU in Austin. He loved it. He then added a couple more classes at a private university in town, and that led to teaching a class at the University of Texas. Before long, he was teaching at all three places. He middle-age pivoted well, to say the least. Me, not so much.

Warning: Whining Ahead.

The combination of Chris's new passion and the boys no longer needing me shook my not-yet-fully-gelled feeling of midlife relevancy and confidence. It reinforced my feeling of not knowing my role in life and created a big void. The kids were independent, Chris was busy, my writing was sporadic, and I no longer knew most of the women in our neighborhood anymore now that the nonstop volunteer demands of the grade school years were over. I suppose I could have been a lunch monitor at the middle school or a crossing guard or bus driver, but good god. I'm not that much of a masochist. It felt like everyone was moving on, and not just in my family. The few mom friends in town that I regularly hung out with went back to work or started new jobs due to either desire or necessity. The complicated stay-at-home mom goes back to working-mom transition is never easy, but once again

I felt like everyone was one step ahead of me, progressing with their lives. I honestly had nothing on my schedule besides writing snarky captions for *Us Weekly*'s Fashion Police once a week. *For free.* Writing jokes about Justin Bieber's most recent pants disaster isn't as satisfying as you'd think. It felt like I was back to where I started as a laid-off copywriter all those years ago when the only group that wanted me was the Marine Corps.

Exacerbating this feeling was the fact that I'd seen other women become completely lost when their kids graduated from high school, and I'd long considered them to be cautionary tales. I wanted to be more like my mom, who'd always worked. When I left for college, she wasn't bereft. Not only did she not sit on my bed and cry, but she immediately took down my posters and turned my childhood bedroom into a Mickey Mouse–themed craft oasis for her sewing projects. It was almost like she'd been counting down the days. Which is healthy! I wasn't that upset! I'm not still holding a grudge that my Prince album collection was replaced by bins of thread! True, my writing and my new friend group and my activism that I'd worked to build ensured that I wasn't completely dependent on my family for my identity, but it clearly wasn't enough. What was an unemployed maxi-pad writer to do?

"You're a little rudderless," Chris said one morning after I told him I was awake at 3 a.m. worrying about paying for college and retirement and calculating how long we could make it before we'd have to start dumpster diving for meals. "You just need to find something to latch onto. Something that's challenging and that keeps you busy. And hopefully that something also comes with a salary because I'm also a little worried about the dumpster meals."

The solutions to that particular identity crisis (my sixth? Seventh?) would eventually include getting a dog and a job. Both weren't super easy to find, and both proved to be slight pains in the ass—mostly our dog, who is by all evidence 90 percent stomach. But I knew I had to do something because I didn't want to end up parked outside a Gymboree blasting "Sunrise, Sunset" from the *Fiddler on the Roof* cast album while yelling "ENJOY IT BECAUSE IT GOES FAST!" at the young mothers walking in. We've all had that woman yell at us. Nobody wants to be that woman.

* * *

Closely related to being invisible is being treated like you're irrelevant. Or condescended to simply because you're older. Let me back up in case you didn't understand that: "condescend" means "talking down to." See? That's how it happens.

When I was young, most people would see a blonde woman from North Dakota dressed like a deranged Sunday School teacher and immediately assume that I was an idiot. That I was basically a giant poodle not smart enough to know how things like airplane seatbelts work. Like once on a flight to Phoenix when a Dockers-clad middle-manager asked if I needed help connecting the two ends of the belt to "make them go clicky." What the hell, man. Actually, now that I think about it, he was probably just a perv who wanted access to my lap. But the point is, it sucks to be underestimated, and it's now happening to me even more.

From what I can tell, there are three ways that middle-aged women are treated by the general public:

1. Ignored completely (bad)
2. Dismissed as "sweet" (worse)
3. Presumed to be an absolute twit who needs help ordering a cold brew kombucha after someone youngsplains to her what cold brew kombucha even is (here's what it is: pretty fucking gross)

The ignored and invisible thing at middle age is its whole own thing (literally—it's like five pages back), and I'll get to the sweet old lady part next, so let's talk about being treated like a complete dumbass. As mentioned, I didn't have to wait until my older years for this to happen because I'm a blonde woman from North Dakota who looks like a background extra from *Little House on the Prairie*. I'm the innocent schoolmarm you see clapping erasers behind Half Pint right before I'm mauled to death by the town bear. You'd think I'd be used to not being taken seriously, but now that I'm (lightly) wrinkled and (somewhat) gray, the condescension has really picked up in frequency. I *hate* it. Just because I was born in the late '60s and have a few AARP tote bags filled with cassette tapes, hard candy, and old *Dynamite* magazines doesn't mean I'm an out-of-touch moron who needs help navigating modern society. And even when it's not meant to be rude, it still stings.

I went to the beautiful downtown Austin library to do some work a while ago, and as soon as I walked into the airy main entrance, the tattooed, pierced, and purple-haired lass behind the desk jumped into my path to happily tell me they had a computer literacy class coming up for "patrons my age."

"What do you mean 'my age'?" I asked with narrowed eyes and a scowl. Holy hell, was I being mistaken for a stupid senior citizen? *Again?* I mentally steeled myself to go on a pissed-off kicking rampage in the Self-Help section if my knees were feeling up to it, but then I looked at the flier she was holding out to me in her young hand and saw that the age listed for the class was fifty-plus. *Dammit.* I was fifty-plus. I just didn't think it was *obvious*. I was insultingly yet accurately profiled.

Once my heart rate returned to normal, I wondered why the library was even offering a class like that to people as young as *moi*. Most people my age know how to use a computer by this point. You're probably living in an actual cave if you don't have basic internet literacy. I mean, no judgment if you are living in a cave, but you're missing out on a lot of great Netflix, you freaky stalactite weirdo. It's true that people my age aren't digital natives like my kids, who sent us texts from the crib demanding midnight bottle service, but we didn't grow up listening to music on a Victrola or sending each other Western Union telegrams about the Wham! concert we went to the other night, either.

"GEORGE MICHAEL LOOKED HOT. STOP. I'M 100 PERCENT SURE HE LIKES GIRLS. STOP. HE IS DEFINITELY NOT GAY. STOP. ANDREW RIDGELEY'S CAREER WILL LAST FOREVER. STOP."

True, I used a word processor in college and sniffed correction fluid for a quick high and only learned e-mail in my late twenties when I primarily used it to send company-wide jokes about my boss's (alleged) hair plug surgery, but I know how to make my iPhone order lunch for crissakes. Even my eighty-year-old dad knows how to send me email attachments from his AOL account. Well, he kind of does. It's sometimes a process.

Those neurotic thoughts and more raced through my mind while the now-wary library clerk cautiously watched me read the flier. I looked a little wan and sweaty, so she may have been looking for signs of cardiac trouble too. Finally, and rather frostily, I thrust the paper back at her and replied, "Thank you, but I am *not* interested." Then, before I grandly flounced away to the library's jigsaw puzzle section to see if there were any new cat ones, I took a second to show off the tech savviness of my generation so that in the future, she knew to not fuck with us.

"Would you like me to post about this fifty-plus computer literacy class on my Instastories or on TikTok? What's the library's hashtag?

Any Twitter analytics I should know about? Oh, and by the way, I have that same Instagram shirt you're wearing—doesn't HoneypotJames39 have such sick designs?"

Obviously, I go to a different branch now.

Of course, it's normal and natural to feel that anyone older than you isn't hep to the latest trends, news, or fashion. I get that because I'm a person using the word "hep" in 2022. And I'm sure I sometimes felt that way about older people when I was younger. Everyone does. It's developmentally correct to think you're stronger and smarter than the olds. I like to think I was a bit more graceful about it, though. At least I hope so. When my mom thought that the hard rock band Molly Hatchet was a woman named Molly Hatchet, I didn't make fun of her. Or when she thought the Bee Gees song "More Than a Woman" was "Bald-Headed Woman." That lady *really* didn't understand a lot of songs.

"Oh, I don't like this one at all, Wendi. Who would write a song about a grease rag? That's just stupid. Nobody likes grease rags that much."

"It's 'Freeze Frame' by The J. Geils Band, Mom."

"That doesn't make any sense, either."

I never said things to my elders like, "You just don't get it, man," like hippie kids in the '60s did to their uptight astronaut dads right before they ran off to join an Oregon sex cult. Rather, I appreciated my elders. The fact that my grandma loved watching *The Lawrence Welk Show* and going to bed at 7 p.m. made sense to me. Stanning a bandleader with a strong Norwegian accent who was surrounded by bubbles and uptight white women named Eleanor certainly wasn't a reason to dismiss Grandma Ollie's years of experience and intelligence. I've always thought that older people know what they know, and younger people know what they know, and sometimes there's a bit of crossing over and you get to benefit from the taste and wisdom of both generations.

Gen X has pretty much seen everything by now. That's why condescending to us doesn't make sense. We have the internet, so we know what's up, what's new, what's happening, and what to avoid. Some of us also own teenagers who, somewhat unwillingly, expose us to the latest shit. My oldest son, Sam, who, as of this writing, is studying music industry in London, regularly plays his favorite songs in the car and asks my opinion. At first, I thought it was nice that he wanted to bond in that way, but I soon realized he just does it because he loves to see my reactions to what is now considered music.

"Do you like this one? It's by Smoke Purp. He has two million followers."

"Oh, my god, is this the explicit version??"

"No, that was the clean version. Okay, how about this one? It's Yung Gravy."

"Is it supposed to sound like someone jackhammering a Nespresso machine?"

"Okay, I think you'll like this one. KingCraz8."

"Do these guys know what a melody is? Any of them? Even one?"

"There's more to life than 'The Piña Colada Song,' Mom."

What I wouldn't give to hear a nice ditty about a grease rag.

I admit to being somewhat out of touch when it comes to music, but I'm not with most other things, which is good because that means when someone treats me like I'm an old dummy, I can usually set them straight. I mean, if I care enough to take the time. But it's also bad that I'm up on the latest stuff because as I get older and my memory isn't as great, I need to be careful to save space in my brain for what's important. Do I want to keep *Game of Thrones* trivia in there just because it helps me make conversation with a twenty-two-year-old barista? Is it worth the risk of forgetting my social security number because those brain cells are occupied with the plot of *Spring Breakers*? Besides appearing relevant to a stranger and fending off condescension, what does knowing shit like the names of all of the Kardashian/ Jenner clan really gain me? Unless my assisted living facility is one day threatened by an evil Eastern European billionaire who'll blow the entire place up if nobody tells him Kim and Kanye's oldest daughter North West's birth date (June 15, 2013), I can probably let that knowledge go and just relax in my rocking chair. It's a dilemma.

Which brings me to the other aspect of age condescension: "Cute Little Old Lady" syndrome. This is when an older person is infantilized and talked about like a child, despite their lifetime of knowledge and accomplishments. I'm not there yet, despite being oldish and, if I'm honest, super cute, but it's not far off. I'll probably need to shrink a bit more to hit the "little" part of it. Maybe develop a hunch, which I'm close to doing anyway from iPhone overuse. Lest you think I'm making this syndrome up, I saw it happen when eighty-one-year-old Jane Fonda was arrested at climate change protests two weeks in a row. She brought her granddaughter to the march and was also joined by her pals Ted Danson and Sam Waterston, both men in their seventies. Now, anyone who speaks up and uses their voice and fights for what's right is pretty badass, no matter who they are. Or how old they are. Still, while most of the online comments were of the "Go Jane!" variety, there were more than a few that called her "adorable." ADORABLE. This is a woman who has lived a long, full, remarkable life, a woman who is still out there marching and yelling about equality, and she's immediately minimized with the same word you'd use to describe a fucking Maltipoo? Would anyone ever call seventy-nine-year-old Bernie Sanders adorable? Well, okay, bad example because he was pretty cute in his mittens. But nobody called Ted or

Sam adorable that day. I checked. Not a single patronizing comment about the men even though they're both senior citizens too. Jane is an octogenarian, yes, but that's no reason to condescend to her. She's still strong, powerful, and vibrant and will be for years. So knock that shit off, youngs. And, while I'm at it, stop doing it to the late Justice Ginsburg too. I saw an atrocious swimsuit sold online that was printed with images of her face all over it. WTF, she was a Supreme Court justice for god's sake, not a Disney character.

There's a popular cross-stitch design I've seen that reads, "Go Ahead, Underestimate Me. This'll Be Fun." As I age and the condescension picks up, that may be my motto going forward. Maybe I am blonde and originally from North Dakota and live in Texas and am a woman, and maybe I'm getting older and cuter and shrinking, but so what? Why not use that to my advantage? I don't mean I'm going to be a little old lady stealing purses out of carts at the grocery store because nobody would ever suspect me. I would never do that. Okay, I probably won't do that. Fine, I might do that because it's called My Retirement Plan.

* * *

But let's go back to being a middle-aged phantom menace in public. I admit that besides the customer service issues, it's not too bad going unnoticed now. In fact, I probably wouldn't go back to being visible if I could. Here's why: The aforementioned lack of unwanted male attention. Yes, it's important when moving heavy furniture, but I've realized that at no other time do I need it. I'm happily married, and even if I wasn't, it's as freeing as a motherfucker to just go about your day as a woman without being noticed or bothered.

The time I most enjoyed being invisible was when I went to Vegas a couple years ago. I was there for the weekend with my friends Melisa and Ann to celebrate Melisa's fiftieth birthday with a Manilow show. (The best way to celebrate anything, and if you disagree, you're wrong, and clearly don't understand #ManilowMagic.) I've been to Vegas probably over one hundred times, and on almost every visit, I've had to deal with some kind of gross male attention. Even when I was with Chris. A wedding ring and an actual husband holding your hand isn't a dealbreaker to a manslob who's been chugging Red Bull and vodka since 7 a.m. and wants to pat your ass "for some good roulette luck." But on this particular middle-aged adventure, we remained completely unbothered. The whole time. Nobody looked twice or even once at us. We could have robbed fifty million dollars from the vault at Caesars Palace because we probably wouldn't even have been visible on the security cams. (Pitch idea: this should be the plot of *Ocean's 50*. Someone tell Clooney and Pitt.) But while it was almost unsettling to walk through the casino floor and get zero attention, it also filled me with a ton of bravado. I felt untouchable. Is that what men feel like all the time? Like they can just take up space unapologetically? I was so pumped up by it that at one point we were walking through the gaming floor at the Bellagio, and I intentionally cut off a bachelor party of drunk cargo short bros just to fuck with them. "Yo, watch it lady, you made me spill my drink!" one of the dinguses holding a four-foot-long neon green margarita yelped.

"Didn't you see me? I was here first. Watch where *you're* going," I sassed back. Damn, it feels good to be a no-longer-capable-of-reproducing gangster.

The three of us made it through that entire weekend, a weekend spent in crowded casinos, bars, and clubs, and the packed strip, a weekend spent laughing and drinking and being weird with no fear of embarrassing ourselves, without a single man approaching us even once. I *loved* it. But then on our last night, our luck ran out like it eventually always does in Vegas. We were in the lobby wearing our matching MANIHO t-shirts waiting for our Uber to take us to Barry's show, and an older man with a cane and a white beard clocked us. "Uh oh," I said to Ann and Melisa in my weary three-pack-a-day ancient gambler voice as we watched him make a slow beeline to our group. "Get ready because we're about to be hit on. I didn't think it would happen, but Vegas is still Vegas, man. Gets ya every time."

"Good evening, ladies," he politely said as he limped up. I admit to feeling a little flattered because I knew we looked sexy and irresistible in the fifteen-dollar t-shirts we'd ordered from the internet to dance to "Copacabana" in. Plus, he was in his seventies, so to him, we were young hotties.

"Yes?" I sighed, like he was the millionth guy to bother us that weekend instead of the first. "How can we help you?"

He then said that he took one look at us and knew we were the perfect people to ask for directions to the Mandalay Bay buffet. Which, of course, we were—take a right after the high limit poker tables—so I really can't blame him for profiling us.

Even if we were just vague woman shapes, not screwable, pass.

CHAPTER EIGHT

I'M WEARING BUSINESS CASUAL NOW

Job hunting at fifty was one of the most humbling things I've ever done—second only to the time I tried on swimsuits at TJ Maxx and didn't realize I had the adhesive crotch protector thing stuck on my shoulder until a loud Texan woman yelled at me when I was leaving the store. "Excuse me, ma'am? Y'all totin' a pantyliner on y'all's body!" But after the four months I spent unsuccessfully applying and interviewing for jobs, four months filled with sly insults, ageism, and general weirdness, I think I'd rather sell off all my possessions on eBay and white knuckle it ten or fifteen more years until my social security kicks in than ever try to find full-time employment again.

I thought looking for work was hard when I was twenty-two years old with a freshly minted film degree from the University of Oregon, proudly strutting around Los Angeles in a polyblend miniskirt suit from The Limited, accessorized with snagged white nylons and a brand-new graduation gift briefcase. But that was easy. That was actually kind of fun. Like the day I had an interview at CBS Television City, the legendary studio on Beverly Boulevard where a lot of famous shows were and are still taped. I got lost trying to find the meeting room, and noticing my frustration, a nice security guard said he'd walk me there. We chatted as we passed offices, hallways, and the usual production activity on our way, but then we came upon the holding pen where the *The Price Is Right* audience members are contained. That sounds weird, but it was a gated area next to the building, filled with a sweaty gaggle of excited, cooped-up fans, all waiting to go on the show in their bright-colored t-shirts that said things like KISS ME BOB and SPAY YOUR PETS. They were calm and quiet as we got near, probably thinking about their Plinko strategy, but then we came into their line of sight and all hell broke loose. They took one look at me, at my security detail, and at my little suit and big hair, and immediately went batshit. People pushed and shoved up to the gate to get closer to me, waving their arms and hands and screaming, "Brooke! Brooke! We love you, Brooke! Are you ever getting back together with Stone?! BROOOOOKE!" It was a full-on Beatlemania riot, and I was Paul just trying to not get tackled by a Midwestern lunatic with a fanny pack. Before it escalated and got any worse, my security friend grabbed me by the elbow and hustled me around the corner to where they could no longer see us. "What was *that*?" I gasped, bending over to put my hands on my white-nyloned knees. "What just happened? And why are they calling me Brooke?"

He scowled in their direction and rolled his eyes. "They think you're Brooke from *The Bold and the Beautiful*. It's one of the shows we tape here."

"Oh!" I said, immediately flattered that my fancy business lady outfit was clearly working for me because I'd been mistaken for a soap star. My mind raced as I debated if I should skip the interview and instead take some acting classes or get into modeling because I obviously had palpable star power—until I was brought to earth by the pale, red-haired, freckled guard when he said, "Yeah, last week those boneheads thought I was Eric Estrada."

Sweaty and shaken, but blonde perm still looking fresh, I then breezed into the conference room filled with bored TV executives, and five minutes later, I had my first job in Hollywood. That's what can happen when you're a young dummy who looks like she just got off a Greyhound from Kansas. In my big, new position, I showed CBS TV pilots to random tourists pulled in off the street, then had them fill out a questionnaire about what they watched so the executives would know if they had a hit or not. It wasn't exactly a glamorous position, and I wasn't exactly on my way to lunch at The Polo Lounge. More like on my way to a lot of quiet introspection after spending weeks watching a pilot called *CLAWS* that was an all-cat version of *Look Who's Talking*. You can thank California's circa-1990 tourists for torpedoing that feline gem before it got any airtime.

My middle-age job hunt years later wasn't so easy. I wasn't mistaken for a soap opera sexpot this time around. I wasn't even mistaken for the crazy soap opera dowager that Stone pushed down the stairs so he and his twenty-year-old wife, Kayleigh, could run off to Bermuda with the insurance money. From start to finish during my recent attempts at getting hired, I was clocked as an older person. I had too much experience, but I also had too little experience. I was overqualified, and I was underqualified. I was a round, wrinkled peg in a square, millennial hole. But mostly, I was pissed-off at myself that I'd taken time off to raise my family, even though it wasn't my choice at first, and the huge gap in my resumé was now biting me in the ass. At least I didn't still have a perm.

The reason I was job hunting at my advanced age was twofold. First, the boys were older and didn't need me or daycare, so I had no reason to still be a stay-at-home mom. Like some kind of European dilettante, I was spending more time at matinees than cooking and cleaning and child-raising. It was fun, but not ideal because the second reason I was job hunting was money. We'd done okay on one income for a long time, but now we had two looming college tuitions, plus our retirement savings needed a few more zeroes if we wanted to avoid having to put on Walmart vests. Nobody really talks about the middle-age pinch of saving for college while also saving for your future, but it isn't easy. Chris had started teaching and it paid less than his former corporate job, and it's not like kids can still pay for school by washing dishes part-time because college tuition has doubled since Sam was born in 2001. NYU now costs eighty-thousand dollars a year, and that doesn't even include a butler and a private jet.

We were also being killed by our health insurance. Relatively speaking. The four of us hardly ever need to go to the doctor (knock on wood), but we paid around eighteen-hundred dollars a month for shitty coverage with a high deductible. That's probably lower than some people pay, but it was still more than our mortgage. "Be careful! We can't afford for you to get hurt!" is a running mantra around our house. A house that includes two teen boys, a husband who bicycles on busy roads every day, and an accident-prone idiot named Wendi who does things like burn her face by dropping frozen chicken into hot grease. Yes, that actually happened, and yes, it was painful, but I will say that once the singed skin fell off, my cheeks looked *amazing*. Much cheaper than a chemical peel at the spa too.

Our insurance payments had become stressful and untenable, so finally, after paying eight-hundred seventy-five dollars to have a suspicious mole frozen off my leg—the same price as a plane ticket to Paris, where I'd still have a suspicious mole but be happily eating cheese and bread and not thinking about said mole—I announced, "Maybe I should get a full-time job that includes better insurance." Then I had to tell Chris to stop dancing around in delight in case he slipped on the tile and needed an ER visit that we couldn't afford without selling a body part.

I embarked on my new job journey with a lot of hope. I had a solid work history, after all. I don't have a medical or law degree, and I was never a CEO or a VP or even an assistant to an assistant manager, but I'd still held fairly decent jobs like network television buyer, literary agent assistant, executive assistant at a major film studio, and copywriter. I'd worked for companies like Warner Bros, E! Entertainment, and The Gersh Agency. Plus, those four days in 1989 that I spent spray painting shelves at the Carson City, Nevada, Kmart because my parents thought I needed to get off the damn couch and "go build some character." The problem was that all of those jobs were all over fifteen years prior.

That said, during my time chained to the oven all day, I'd still managed to do some freelance writing for clients like the LPGA, Merrill Lynch, and General Mills, thanks to my blog connections. I wasn't *completely* out of the loop. So I put together an online writing portfolio to replace my outdated leather-bound one gathering dust up in the attic—oh, how I'd loved walking into meetings with that portfolio—and updated my resumé. The resumé proved challenging when my faulty middle-aged memory tried to recall the past twenty years in chronological order. (Start writing things down when you're thirty, people.) I then signed up for LinkedIn, Indeed, GetMeAFuckingJob.com, and the rest of the online employment databases that seem easy but are really a huge pain in the ass. Do I need twenty alerts a day about offshore drilling jobs in my area? No, I do not. And while I wasn't thinking too much about the hindrance of my age during all of this prep, I intentionally left about a third of my experience and the year I graduated from college off my resumé. That was maybe a little paranoid, but I'd heard chatter about employment ageism, and I was also watching the show *Younger* at the time. If you haven't seen it, it's about a woman who lies about her age to get a job in publishing. I'd never be able to do that because my elbows are too wrinkled, and also the jig would be up as soon as someone brought up '80s trivia and I screamed out the name of every woman in Bananarama (Sara! Siobhan! Keren!). I didn't like omitting my history, but I also didn't think it was worth the risk of being prejudged.

Now I know that maybe if I'd mentioned that I graduated from college in 1990, I wouldn't have suffered being interviewed by people who were *born* in 1990.

The good news is my resumé worked well enough to score a few meetings. The bad news is that I only made it about two seconds into my first interview before I realized that things had changed in the years since I'd been off the market. Like, *a lot.* That's to be expected with the younger generation hitting the workforce, and technology advancing, and white dude bros now making millions from apps that deliver food, sex, and cat litter 24/7, but still.

The first interview I landed was for an in-house writing position at a downtown Austin marketing agency. I thought I was perfect for it with my fifteen-plus years of copywriting experience and the good work in my portfolio. However, my first clue that this job wasn't the right fit should have been that the agency describes itself as "Data Driven. Viral Optimized. Growth Focused." Quite the lofty description for a place that produces things like fliers for Laffy Taffy and second-tier dog food. Are you changing humanity for the better with lines like "Laff Your Taff Off," Chad? A quick look at their work and website told me that their whole vibe was white guy bravado bullshit, something I've seen plenty of in my more than fifty years on earth and something I avoid like the plague. Still, much like a woman dating a guy for his money, I was a woman willing to interview for health insurance.

My meeting with the agency wasn't in-person, even though I live just eight miles from their office, but on Zoom. This was prepandemic, so kind of an odd choice back then. But I prepared for the call by opening the blinds and turning on a few lamps in my home office because I know that like Angela Lansbury and naked mole rats, I look best in either super bright light or total blackness. Gotta play to your strengths. The call began at the appointed time, and six thirty-year-olds sitting in a sad, dim conference room popped onto on my laptop screen. My memory of the interview is a bit fuzzy, but I seem to recall that everyone was either named "Chrisalee" or "The Tankster." The self-important, blonde-bobbed HR woman, Chrisalee, peppered me with typical HR questions for a few minutes, then she dropped the "omg it's so obvious from looking at her wrinkled face that she's ancient" hammer by casually asking, "In your decades of creative work, have you ever . . ."

She fucking decaded me, man.

As if that wasn't enough humiliation, Blonde Bob then proceeded to do a lightning round of platforms and apps the agency uses and asked if I was proficient in them. Is this some kind of oldie test? I wondered. And were there really now that many new platforms and apps that I didn't know about? Or did she make them up? I'm pretty tech-savvy, but I honestly hadn't heard of a single one she mentioned. Still, I'm a typical Gen Xer who just goes along with whatever to get the job, so I faked it. It went something like this:

"Do you know Wizzywag?"

"Yep."

"Dinoplumpa"?

"Of course."

"PaddyWick?"

"Who doesn't?"

"Mfoomy?"

"I can't get enough Mfoomy. It's viral-optimized my data-driven growth focus in a million ways."

At that point, I saw the oldest The Tankster in the room crack a smile because he knew I was being a bit of a jerk, but then came the ultimate You're an Oldie question. Blonde Bob Chrisalee threw a serious look on her face and asked, "How would you handle being a mentor to all of the younger employees?" I wanted to reply, "Not well, bitch, because they can fucking figure things out by themselves like I did when I worked for cokehead movie producers who threw staplers at my head," but instead, I mumbled something about learning as much from them as they do me, like you say when you adopt a blind shelter dog and post about it on Instagram. Mercifully the inquisition then ended before she could ask what I had in common with Grandma Moses and Methuselah. They all said goodbye, that they'd get back to me, and I said, "thank you" and slammed the lid of my laptop down like I was putting out a fire. It was only 10 a.m., but I still went to the kitchen and poured myself a decades of experience glass of wine.

Later, I fantasized about asking the preschoolers if they were proficient in a few things.

"Are you skilled in fax machine?"

"Beeper?"

"Interoffice memos?"

"Do you know what a stamp is?"

"What's your CB radio handle? Do you copy, Chrisalee? That's a big ten-four, buddy. We got Smokey on our tail."

To add insult to injury, the agency later asked me to take a timed writing test where I had to "craft" a marketing email about Valentine's Day and dog food. That sexy combination. Even though I thought it was stupid and beneath my level of experience, I sucked it up and did it because I really wanted a job. I thought my work was solid until the brusque, young president of the agency video-called me from Finland, where he was probably buying reindeer pelts to turn into yoga mats, and told me that I didn't quite "capture the soul of the product." Again, the product was dog food for Valentine's Day. Does kibble have a soul? My dog, Teddy, hasn't ever mentioned a spiritual experience with his bowl of Purina.

I began to miss my job spray-painting shelves at the Carson City Kmart.

Not long after that "Data Driven. Viral Optimized. Growth Focused" humiliation, I signed up for even more kicks to the balls when I went to an interview at a big, high-tech employer north of Austin. It was in-person this time and not on Zoom, so I had to worry more about finding an interview outfit that didn't look fresh from the '90s than about my lighting. The job I was up for was social media manager, something I'm good at because of my freelance work and my blog. I was there at the start of Twitter, mind you, back in those #NikonHatesBabies days, so I thought I was a real contender. Unfortunately, my experience didn't seem to impress the seven people I met with that day. Yes, seven people. What's with the interviewing in packs these days, millennials? Is it because you grew up with "circle time"? Is it like everybody in the place gets a vote on which idiot to hire now? I'm not saying that's a bad thing. I certainly don't want to go back to the days when I interviewed for a Hollywood assistant job alone in the Hollywood boss's house (and was grateful that he didn't go full Harvey Weinstein on me because that could have happened), but still. A few more people in that conference room asking me about my life and work and it would have been a grand jury.

The people I met with that day were all born when I was in my mid-twenties and starting my career, which is fine and to be expected. Most people my age who didn't take a child-raising hiatus are now CEOs and VPs, not doing flunky interviews. They were nice and polite to me, yet there was definitely a hint of condescension in the air. And I'm really good at picking up hints of condescension—ask any Clinique counter worker who's ever tried to sell me a skin care regimen. Only now do I realize that it probably felt weird to consider me as their equal or even their subordinate. I probably seemed more like their mother or aunt sitting there than I did a potential co-worker—mostly when I said things like, "I remember when social media didn't exist, and we had to call people on the phone to tell them we think their shoes are ugly. Hahaha! You should follow me on the 'gram." I probably didn't seem like a peer or someone who'd be interested in joining their softball team or in going out for drinks or the types of things co-workers in their twenties and thirties do. And they were right, I wouldn't want to do any of that. When Chris worked in an office full of younger people, they regularly asked him to join them in horrifying group social activities like axe-throwing night and "midnight bike ride jams."

"I'd rather stay home on the couch with a nice glass of pinot and watch *Barnaby Jones*," he told me. "Not drink cheap beer and ride a fixed-gear bike in the dark. I did enough of that thirty years ago. And why do they all bring their untrained dogs into the office? Last week Li'l Peanut destroyed the snack supply."

The interview was a weird dynamic for all of us involved, so not surprisingly, I didn't get the job. Or at least I don't think I did because instead of them telling you you're not hired, you're now just ghosted like a bad Tinder date. Too bad for them, though, considering that at my age I probably count toward their diversity stats. I'm sure a fifty-year-old female checks more than a few boxes on the old EEOC form. Maybe they were worried I'd need a wheelchair ramp in a few years after I break a hip trying to dislodge a paper jam in the printer.

I can't entirely blame any of the people I interviewed with for my failed job hunt. There was probably a bit of self-sabotage happening too. Did I try to get hired as hard as I should have tried? Maybe, maybe not. I definitely wanted insurance, but I really didn't want an 8 a.m. to 5 p.m. office job. Driving an hour each way, only to sit in a cubicle all day, sounded awful. I'd spent almost twenty years working from home in my pajama bottoms. For me, spending time in an office would be like a lifelong bachelor with horrible solitary habits trying to cohabitate with his new bride. "What do you mean I can't just leave my empty dishes on my desk for three weeks? No, I didn't know I shouldn't cook fish in the microwave. Seriously, none of you take TV breaks in the middle of the workday? How do you keep up with *The Chew*?" I'm also well past the point of ever taking arbitrary deadlines seriously, which isn't a desirable quality in an employee. I know for a fact that nobody will die if Emily T. doesn't get her analytics report to Emily P. by the fourth of the month. If you're not a brain surgeon or landing the space shuttle, calm the fuck down with your "work emergencies." Know what a real emergency is? Holding a baby that's puking down your back in one arm while you help your toddler with diarrhea wipe himself with the other, not the stupid weekly metrics report.

There's a famous story about legendary actress Shelley Winters that may or may not be true. I hope it's true. Late in her life, decades into an accomplished career, she was asked to audition for a project. And, as if that wasn't disrespectful enough, she was told to be sure to bring along her headshot and resumé. She arrived at the casting office carrying a huge carpetbag. When asked if she'd brought her photo and resumé for them as requested, she opened her bag, took out her first Academy Award and, placing it on the table before them, said, "Here's my photo." Then she took out her second Oscar, placed that on the table too, and said, "And here's my fucking resumé."

Every interview I had was truly humbling. So was not even hearing back from the many other jobs I applied to. Most of them had titles I didn't even understand too, like "Virtual Experience Officer" and "Director of Online Audience Profiling." What's a "Director of Movement Trendology" and why does it exist in a suburban dental office? I'm still not sure if those are real or just made-up positions that sound cool. Years ago, I met a slick, charming Austin guy who carried business cards that said he was Matthew McConaughey's "VP of Keepin' It Real," but that actually was a legitimate job for a charming Austin guy.

"Is this shirt keeping it real?"

"No, Matt, try another one on."

Employment indignities when you're over forty are hardly unique to me. It's a common experience shared by us olds. That's why there are plenty of ageism lawsuits, stories about men getting Botox to look younger in the job market, and fifty-five-year-old women taking on internships where they have to fetch coffee for their zygote boss, the CEO of an online yoga influencer agency.

But no matter how old you are, job rejection is a big blow to the ego. It really stings when you know you're still youthful and you have a lot to contribute. It can be discouraging and frustrating to feel like you're no longer relevant. I finally put my job hunt on hold after a few months of trying and not getting anywhere.

Then one morning at 4 a.m., my usual time to be wide awake questioning my life choices, I had flashback. And not a good one. I remembered that when I was in my thirties and working as a copywriter at the downtown Austin agency, I was asked to interview an older woman who was returning to work after raising kids. My ponytailed art director partner, Steve, and I looked through her portfolio filled with ads and clippings she'd written, and instead of noticing if they were good or not, we noticed that they were yellowed with age and created for businesses that were no longer around. That was an immediate problem because ad agencies, and the both of us at the time, place a great importance on new, new, new. We talked with this woman a bit, told her about the agency, then nicely said goodbye. At least I hope I was nice and not condescending. Then, when our boss asked how it went, we both shrugged and said, "Good, I guess. But she's too old." I know. I KNOW. Dear god, I know. I was a complete asshole.

I was horrified when I remembered. That woman was probably only in her mid-forties at the time, maybe even younger, and I dismissed her outright. Why? She was no threat to me. It certainly wouldn't have been a big deal to suggest that she interview with my boss. I've thought about it a lot and honestly wish I knew her name so I could reach out and apologize for my actions that day—and also to say that I'm sorry that it took the shoe being on the other foot for me to finally realize that what I did was wrong and prejudiced. But maybe that's always the way? Not to excuse my behavior, but maybe the brashness of youth disappears only to be replaced by the humbleness of middle age? The only redeeming part of this story is that at least I didn't ask her if she knew how to use Wizzywag and Mfoomy.

A few months after resigning myself to just plod along with my regular freelance work, a friend put me up for a social media position at a large nonprofit. This time, all it took was one proposal and one phone call, and boom. I was hired. Sight unseen too because nobody needed a video call to check me out. Nor was there any jumping through hoops, or "how would you mentor?" or "fill out this twenty-page online application that will make your computer freeze up" stuff. Yes, I was qualified for the job, but I'd also been qualified for the ones I'd interviewed for too. I'd been more than qualified. The difference this time was that the friend who gave me the lead is my age, the woman who hired me is my age, and most of my co-workers are women over the age of forty. And they all know that if I made it this far in life, I'm way too tired to cause trouble, play office politics, or ask people to support me in a 5K Fun Run. Most of my friends have gotten jobs this way too, so it looks like the good ol' boys network maybe now has a benevolent parallel good ol' ladies network.

I've now been at my nonprofit job for a few years, working part-time on my own schedule from home, and I like it. I can wear pajamas and take my regular afternoon TV break to catch up on *The Chew*. I have time for the boys, who still need me more than they let on. College applications are no joke. And it's nice to have something else in my life where I feel valued, appreciated, and trusted for my experience. I'm no longer rudderless because I'm doing good work for a good cause with good people. The only downside to my job is that it didn't come with health insurance, but that's okay. The good ol' ladies don't organize axe-throwing nights.

FERRIS BUELLER'S LAID OFF

It's a beautiful spring day in suburban Chicago, and fifty-year-old Ferris Bueller decides he just can't deal with going into work.

"I'm not well," he tells his admin over the phone. "I threw my back out sneezing." She believes it because she's twenty-five-years-old and knows elderly men like him are easily injured. Ferris's uptight teenage daughter Jeannie then walks into the room and rolls her eyes when she sees him still in bed. "Can't adult today? Bite the big 1" she texts from two feet away. He gives her an innocent smile. She texts him a middle finger emoji.

Once home alone, Ferris tweets, "They bought it!" to his twelve-hundred @FerrisWheel followers. "This is my 9th sick day this quarter. If I go for 10, I'll have to barf up a lung." Then he remembers that two of his friends from high school recently died of lung disease caused by thirty-five years of smoking, and he posts an inspirational meme on Instagram that says, "Life Moves Pretty Fast. If You Don't Stop to Look Around Once in a While, You Could Miss It." His neighbor immediately comments, "Up yours snowflake #MAGA."

Ferris calls his best friend, Cameron, who's clinically depressed despite retiring at age thirty because he bought Apple stock in 1984. "Want to hang out today?" Ferris asks. "I'm playing hooky from work."

Cameron replies, "When Cameron was in Egypt's land, let my Cameron gooooo . . . wait, was that culturally insensitive? I never know anymore. But bro, you've had three written warnings from human resources. Maybe you should spend today on LinkedIn."

Meanwhile, there's confusion on the weekly staff call when Ferris doesn't join in. "Is Marketing on the line?" asks the team leader. "Bueller? Bueller? Bueller?"

"I heard he passed out at 31 Flavors last night," someone says, which is surprising because everyone knows Ferris is on the Keto diet due to his high blood pressure. They start a GoFundMe page.

Word gets to Mr. Rooney, the head of HR, that Ferris called in sick again. His admin shrugs and says, "Everyone here loves him, Ed. Sportos, Motorheads, Geeks, Sluts, Bloods, Wastoids, Dweebies, Dickheads. They all think he's a righteous dude."

Mr. Rooney stares at her in horror because she pretty much just violated the entire company handbook and vows to bust Ferris.

Cameron and Ferris drive to the office in one of ten vintage Ferraris that Cameron bought to fill his existential void and break Ferris's ex-wife, Sloane, out by phoning in a bogus story about her dead grandmother. Sloane gets in the car and says, "My grandma died thirty years ago, and I'm a senior VP who can leave whenever I like, you morons. Honestly, it's shit like this that made me divorce your ass ten years ago, Ferris. And take off that beret. You look like an idiot." She still goes to Chicago with them because they're not as bad as the losers she's seen on Bumble recently.

After the threesome drop the Ferrari off at a parking garage, the attendant takes it out for a joyride not knowing it's being tracked by GPS. He will later be fired, and Cameron will sue the garage owner into devastating ruin. Ohhhh, yeahhhhh, Chick-chikahhhhh.

Sloane wants to visit Sears Tower, but they pass when they realize it's now called Willis Tower and it costs twenty-four-ninety-nine each to ride the elevator. "What a racket," Ferris says. "Back in my day, it was only five dollars." Sloane reminds him that "back in his day" was thirty-two years ago, and then they all quietly contemplate their impending deaths.

Next, they head to a fancy restaurant but can't get a table, so Ferris tells the *maitre d'* that he's the "Sausage King of Chicago." The *maitre d'* says, "Nice try, sicko, but Abe Froman died from a massive heart attack twenty years ago." They eat a sad meal at a vegan food truck in the alley.

Back in the suburbs, Rooney arrives at Ferris's house and is kicked in the face by Jeannie, who was sent home after being caught using a Juul in the school bathroom. She calls the police and says she has a "*To Catch a Predator* sitch" happening but not to worry because she's filming it all on her iPhone. The cops still drag her to the police station where a cute junkie flirts with her. "Gross, back off, dude," she tells him. "I'd never date a mediocre white druggie like you. I'm way too busy fighting the patriarchy."

After bitching about the streets being closed due to yet another ethnic pride parade, Ferris climbs onto a float and lip-synchs "Twist and Shout" because it's on his bucket list. Sloane and Cameron enjoy his performance until they remember that two of the four Beatles are dead, and so are most of their musical heroes, and now everything on the radio is an auto-tuned song about butts. Then Ferris leaves the float to buy some extra-strength Motrin because twisting was not so good for his lower back.

On their way home, Ferris sees he has thirty missed messages from work, so he calls an Uber to speed him to the office. He makes it to his desk right before Rooney comes in and tells him, "While you were out, the partners and I took a hard look at your job performance."

Ferris sighs. "Well, I guess that means I'm fired. I probably deserve it due to years of not taking my job seriously, not showing up, and finding loopholes and cheats to get ahead over way more deserving people."

"Are you kidding me?" Rooney answers. "You're a white man in America. We're giving you a promotion!"

"I said it before and I'll say it again," Ferris later tells his friends on Facebook Live. "Life moves pretty fast. If you don't stop to look around once in a while, you could miss it." Then he hacks into the company's financial files and transfers two million dollars into his offshore account.

We Can't Ask Your Age in This Job Interview, but Please Take This Quiz about Rotary Phones

Per the human resources department and the federal government, it's illegal to ask a job candidate their age because it may lead to discrimination. We carefully consider all candidates, no matter the year they were born, when hiring new talent. After all, age is just a number!

But, to help us get to know you better, please fill out this questionnaire that is not at all about your possible irrelevance in a modern office.

1. Where were you when JFK died?
2. Do you know what a SASE is?
3. Is it ever OK to use a smiley-face emoji?
4. Follow-ups: Do you know where to find a smiley-face emoji? If someone used a skull emoji, would you feel afraid?
5. Please describe what the words "Milli Vanilli" mean to you. (essay)
6. How many spaces after a period?

(a) One

(b) Two

If you answered (b), stop filling out this questionnaire immediately. We'll be in touch.

7. What kind of phone did you have as a teenager?

(a) Cell

(b) Trimline push button

(c) Rotary

If you answered (c), stop filling out this questionnaire immediately. We'll be in touch.

8. Does the phrase "I didn't get the memo" inspire wistful memories of getting high from sniffing mimeographs?

9. How upset would you be if a co-worker spilled coffee on your Eileen Fisher cardigan? (essay)

10. When a junior executive gives his thoughts in a meeting, you:

(a) Listen raptly

(b) Congratulate him on his insight

(c) Marvel at how much he resembles a young Mark Harmon

11. If you decide to relive your high-school athletics glory days by fielding for the company softball team without stretching first, will you need:

(a) Possible medical attention

(b) A Motrin day off

(c) A resulting surgery that pushes the limits of our company's feeble healthcare plan

12. Write down the lyrics to "We Are the World."

13. Is "Slack" your preferred business-communication platform or an abridged way to describe the zeitgeist attitude of your twenties?

14. What is your greatest weakness? Is it Simon Le Bon?

15. When paying for business lunches, are you willing to use your AARP discount?

16. Describe a significant challenge you've had to overcome and how an episode of *Oprah* helped you resolve it. (essay)

17. Have you ever typed the words "Help me, I can't get off mute"?

18. How many presidents have been under FBI investigation in your lifetime?

19. Where do you see yourself in five years? Are there palm trees and water aerobics?

20. Our ideal candidate has five-to-seven years of relevant experience. Add up all your previous working years and write down the total.

If you had to use a calendar and a calculator, stop filling out this questionnaire immediately. We'll be in touch.

CHAPTER NINE

I'M WEARING WRINKLES NOW (OR AM I?)

I took my friend Jessica with me the first time I got Botox. Well, "took" is the wrong word because she insisted that she come along to make sure "those freaks don't fuck shit up on your face." She sounds like she's an inmate at a women's maximum security correctional facility, but she's not. She's a cosmetic procedure aficionado. So much so that she regularly gets handwritten "We appreciate your business!" cards from fancy med spas. Once a downtown doctor even sent her a fruit basket to thank her for buying so much Juvéderm. I guess that's one way to get more vitamin C into your diet.

I should explain why I was even doing something so expensive and vain as injecting poison into my forehead in the first place. You see, in my late forties, I realized that I was a troll. Not one of those cute trolls with the Don King–style pink hair that doesn't wear pants, the ones you put on the top of your pencils back in grade school. No, I was more like a disgusting, wart-covered Grimm's Fairy Tale troll that lives under a bridge and terrifies the townsfolk with riddles.

"Before you cross into the village, fair maiden, first you must solve my riddles three. Tell me, what has many eyes but cannot see?"

"Leave me alone, you middle-aged troll! Your ravaged face is hurting my eyes! You're a monster! A monster! Go back to the '80s where you belong! Also, not to criticize, troll, but did you get that riddle from the back of a sugar cereal box? I mean, for fuck's sake, it's not exactly MENSA quality, and you shouldn't be eating empty carbs at your age if you don't want to develop diabetes."

"POTATO. THE ANSWER IS POTATO. LEAVE ME ALONE."

One of the biggest rubs in aging is that you feel more confident than you've ever felt before—until you look in the mirror. At least that's what happened to me. Starting a few years ago, I'd pop out of the shower, glance at my reflection, and then do a startle jump when I saw a wizened crone looking back at me. I'd wonder if a creature from *Lord of the Rings* had sneaked in through an open window. Who is *that*? Is that *me*? Did I always have jowls? And what's going on with my nose? Is it getting larger? Oh, right, I read once that noses grow as you age so I should have had that nose job back when I had my deviated septum surgery in the '90s, but I liked my nose then and guess it's too late now, so *way to go*, Wendi. And on and on and on until I'd be shivering and need a shot of vodka to warm me up. There was a huge disconnect between how I felt—youthful and energetic—and what I thought I looked like whenever I saw myself: Gerard Depardieu.

By my late forties, I'd accepted that I wasn't getting much attention. The whole invisible thing was in full swing by then, and that was fine. It was a relief to not primp and fuss just so I would look attractive enough to prevent random men in a restaurant from yelling, "Watch it, you ugly crone!" when I bumped into their table. I didn't give a shit about that. And my husband Chris has always been, and still is, super complimentary about my looks. Like really complimentary. Like maybe a little too much sometimes. He's kind of like a pageant mom who's always saying things like, "How's my beautiful girl? You're looking good today, missy! Give it a twirl!" It's sweet, and I'm lucky that someone thinks I'm pretty, but even that didn't shut up my inner critic.

Middle age gives you more insight into who you are, but unfortunately, you probably no longer *look* like who you are. That's not me being judgy. It's biology. Your body is aging. Skin is wrinkling, hair is graying, waists are disappearing, and it happens in the blink of a puffy eye. One minute you're Jennifer Lawrence, the next minute you're Lawrence Welk. (I'm assuming anyone who's read this far gets that hip reference.) Of course, I know I'm still attractive in a senior cougar sort of way, but the being-checked-out-on-the-street stuff I used to get? Once I hit forty-five, it disappeared as quickly as my crush on John Travolta did when I heard he believes in volcano aliens. Now I'm either not noticed at all, or I'm looked at like something that just crawled out of the crypt and into Chico's for resort casual wear.

It can be painful to see myself in a photo or even just glance in the mirror now and notice new wrinkles that weren't there the day before. Some mornings I hardly recognize the face staring back at me in the mirror. I don't feel grumpy and tired on the inside, but I looked like I was grumpy and tired on the outside, and I constantly grappled with doing something about my skin before it got worse. But unfortunately, the more I do, the more I need to do, and I know I'm not the only one. Middle-aged women are like tweens who put on makeup to look older, only we're putting on false eyelashes and plumping our smile lines with fillers to look younger. We pay for products and services that claim to reverse aging even though we fully realize that's not possible unless you're riding shotgun in a jacked-up time-traveling DeLorean. (Fun fact: Michael J. Fox is now sixty-one years old.) It's madness.

I don't know for sure, but I think most middle-aged women panic about this. In your forties, beauty treatments become less about glamour and more about maintenance. I haven't gone to a spa for relaxation for years; I go for repair work. And every single time I'm lying on that table, making small talk with the woman who's rubbing battery acid onto my face, I feel like an idiot. I'm a married humor writer who mostly stays home, so why even bother? I think. It's not like I'm on Tinder or *Love Connection*. Should I just embrace my age already? Should I stop covering my grays? Should I not use makeup or use filters? Should I take a stand and fight against unrealistic beauty standards because I know it's bullshit to cater to the male gaze (which isn't even looking in my direction in the first place)?

It's a real problem and my generation may have it worse than any other.

And I blame Steve Jobs.

Hear me out. Steve contributed many good things to the world, but he also invented the iPhone. That means I can text my mom GIFs of sloth babies from an airplane, but it also means that I now see nonstop unflattering cell phone pictures of myself all the damn day. Picture after picture after picture. Everything is now documented with a quick cell phone photo that's then shared with the world. Lunch with a friend? Let's take a photo! At a theme park with kids? Let's take a family photo! Too many glasses of boxed wine while half-naked on the couch watching Hallmark movies but still feeling kind of cute? Let's take a selfie to post on Instagram then wake up in a cold-sweat panic at 3 a.m. to delete! There are more photos of me from the last five years of my life than the first forty-five. Why the hell did technology have to wait until my creeping decrepitude to advance?

I've been camera shy my entire life, but it used to be a lot easier to avoid having my picture taken. The odds that I'd go somewhere and it'd be documented on film were slight. First, someone had to have a loaded camera on them, then ask me to pose. I'd agree, then they'd make sure the pose was perfect and that I was smiling before they pushed the button because they didn't want to "waste film." Next, they had to finish the roll, which could take weeks, especially if it was thirty-six-exposure, drive it to the drugstore, fill out an envelope, wait five to seven days, drive back to the drugstore, and finally call me on my home phone and arrange a time to meet so I could see the developed pictures. And if I didn't like the photos because I had red eyes and a stupid smile in every single one? I'd just rip them in half and toss them in the garbage. Easy peasy. There was no panicking about unflattering pics being emailed or posted online or printed onto a commemorative blanket to give to my parents at Christmas because all photographic evidence of my idiocy was easy to destroy. There weren't files or screenshots or digital evidence to haunt you forever back then. One year I trashed an entire twenty-four double pack of photos from spring break because my blonde perm and Top Ramen diet made me look like Fat David Lee Roth. And good luck finding any pictures of me from junior high because I made sure those nightmares were destroyed long ago. (Fun fact: David Lee Roth was an EMT in New York City for a few years. If I had a heart attack and Diamond Dave showed up, I'd probably sing a few lines of "Hot for Teacher" and then have another heart attack.)

Another way Steve Jobs laid waste to my self-worth is via the iPhone's front-facing camera. There's nothing, *nothing* in the world more frightening than clicking a button on your phone and then unexpectedly seeing your own funhouse face staring back at you. Sweet baby Jesus, my unfiltered, badly lit, and ravaged face live on the tiny screen in my hand is probably the biggest trauma I've ever experienced. And I lived through both the Northridge earthquake and Trump's presidency. Rationally, I know that the image I see may not be accurate—it probably isn't—but that doesn't matter because it's beyond disturbing. Do I really look like THAT? Too bad Jobs didn't think to put an emergency warning system in place, like some kind of tornado siren.

WHOOP WHOOP WHOOP YOU HAVE ACTIVATED THE HOBGOBLIN PHOTO SETTING. PLEASE STEP AWAY FROM THE PHONE IMMEDIATELY OR YOUR EGO WILL BE STOMPED LIKE A NARC AT A BIKER RALLY. WHOOP WHOOP THIS IS AN EMERGENCY. BITCH, I'M SERIOUS.

Regularly seeing my face in photos threw me for a loop. I guess I wasn't used to looking at myself that often in the past. Before long, my image in the photos started to feel more real than my image in the mirror. Or my actual face. When I looked at the pictures, my gaze was never drawn to my smile or to my hair, even if those happened to look good. I didn't even really look at the people I was with in the photos. Or at the, ahem, Universal Studios mascots I posed with because Minions are, like, super cute. Rather, starting at around age forty-five, whenever I studied photos of myself, my eyes immediately focused on my flaws. I thought I had many, but the worst one? The two one-inch creases between my eyebrows. I'd come down with the dreaded "elevens." They're called that because if I traced those wrinkled lines with a Sharpie, you'd see a giant number eleven on my face. And maybe sporting a giant eleven is cool if you're a twenty-year-old whose whole brand is dumbass face tattoos, but no thanks. I don't want fucking *math* on my face. I don't want to be the human answer to "What is ten plus one?" It made me look crabby even when I wasn't.

I've read that elevens are caused by a lifetime of furrowing your brow and squinting, so that tracks. There are baby pictures of me with a furrowed brow, like I had deep concerns about the blocks I was trying to stack. Some women are lucky and only get one line or crease between their eyes, like my friend Meredith. She calls it her "credit card slot." I've wondered if the fact that she has one fewer line between her eyebrows than I do means she's scowled 50 percent less in her lifetime. Maybe. She definitely scowled the night we were in a bar, and I pretended to buy a drink and then swiped my Mastercard between her eyes and said, "Transaction completed." Won't be doing that again.

I tried to blow off my concerns about my elevens, thinking, "I'm not a vain person" and "I'm not one of those women who wears lipstick to the grocery store and perfume to the gym," and "Why not look like Georgia O'Keeffe? She's cool." But then I'd glance at my face and once again focus on the two lines between my eyes. The first and most obvious way to get rid of them was by throwing a bunch of money at my skincare routine, so I booked pricey facials and chemical peels and bought whatever expensive crap the millennial spa women tried to sell me after they crushed my ego with a passive-aggressive insult or two. The comments those spa women make are rough. It's like being pecked to death by duckbill smiles.

"I'm almost done with the pomegranate blueberry goddess glycolic hyperacid follicle application, Mrs. Aarons. How are you feeling?"

"Confused because I think you called me 'creepy' a few minutes ago."

"Oh, no, Mrs. Aarons! I said that your forehead skin is really 'crêpey.' Not creepy."

"Like that's any better? Like I'm a papier-mâché?"

"You're so youthful looking everywhere else that I recommend you try our new organic crystal lactic acid diamond moisturizer to stay that way. It costs more than your car, but this product will stop the cellular action on your forehead from progressing. Would you like me to put a jar of it aside for you? Or do you want to wait until next time when things will be even worse?"

"Just fucking do it, Madyson."

Alas, after a few years of the expensive treatments and applications and products, there wasn't much I gained besides the frequent flier points accumulated from charging it all to my Southwest Airlines credit card. My skin would be softer and brighter after a treatment but only temporarily. No chemical is strong enough to stop the natural aging process. At least not one that's legal in the United States. (Hit me up, you fast and loose South American chemists!) Not only did I still see my elevens, the lines were getting deeper every minute. The day when I couldn't even enjoy professional pictures of myself from an event where I'd won an award because all I saw was my lines was when I knew it was time to finally bite the bullet. What was the alternative? Scotch tape? A headband? Two hundred Instagram filters? No more scowling and fretting? Or, gasp, *fucking self-acceptance?* Please. Those are all stupid ideas, especially that last one. I decided it was finally time to pay someone to inject me with the poison that makes cans of peas burst at the seam.

I didn't have to look far to find a place to get Botox because Austin is a very affluent city. Silicone, Juvéderm, and Botox flow through the streets like chemically enhanced rivers. It's no longer the weird Texas town we moved to twenty years ago because the influx of rich people has made it more Los Angeles fancy than Eugene, Oregon, hippie. The part of town where we live has plenty of multimillion-dollar homes (not mine), and with them come women who are no strangers on ways to look "well rested." There's a Botox joint on every corner, so it wasn't hard to find a med spa. Still, because I'm a budget-conscious person, I first looked on Groupon to see if I could find a bargain. Bad idea. If I'm going to trust someone to paralyze part of my face, I'm not doing it via a forty-five-dollar deal at Rhonda's Face & Doughnut Palace. Or in the back room of a dentist's office. I've seen enough episodes of *Botched* to know that it's never smart to penny-pinch with cosmetic procedures or you could end up like that woman in Tijuana who now has a pound of cement in her ass. So I ended up booking an appointment at the premier dermatology/cosmetic juggernaut in Austin, just like I knew I would.

Westlake Dermatology is located in a huge, white Mediterranean building down the road from me. It's gorgeous and majestic, and I wish I could drape myself in a caftan and live there permanently with my butler Giorgio and my pet capuchin monkey Li'l Giorgio. It definitely stands out on a street that has nothing else going on besides a BBQ shack and a discount fireworks stand. I've always called it "The Pimple Palace," but it's definitely not the first floor's teenage acne treatments or my annual mole patrol with my dermatologist that pays the rent. ("Is a suspicious mole a mole that buys one-way airplane tickets?" I always ask my doctor and then she pretends to laugh and tells me how many barnacles are on my back.)

I arrived at The Pimple Palace the day of my appointment with a nervous stomach. I had cold feet because Botox is botulism and therefore poison and therefore a little scary. It's also expensive. The price I was quoted for one session was three-hundred dollars, however "that could change depending on what the doctor recommends." Yikes. What if he took one look at my face and recommended a thousand dollars? Or two-thousand dollars? I have retirement and college and wine to pay for! "Sorry, Sam, but I blew your tuition check so I could look a few months younger for Instagram, I hope you'll understand." But I got it together, parked my Volvo, walked into the building, and headed up to level two to check in. I didn't think the cosmetic floor would be that different from the dermatology floor, but as soon as I set foot on the marble pathway, I was greeted by a cavalcade of employees who looked like models from Futureland. Their faces were flawless, dewy, and plump in the right places. "Somebody's getting high on their own supply," I chuckled to myself while a woman who was either twenty or eighty years old checked me in. I didn't see a single elevens or credit card slot on anyone's face in the entire joint, so that reassured me. I then tried to relax in the posh waiting area by reading a glossy real estate magazine in which all the houses have wine cellars and panic rooms, until a shadow fell in front of me and I heard a soft voice say, "Hey, hoe bag." Jessica had arrived.

I've known Jessica for at least ten years now, and that's also how many years younger than me she is. The younger generations are a lot more used to the idea of Botox and the like, so she started doing all of that shit when she was in her thirties. As a preventative measure, she says. I recently heard that women in their twenties are now trying to "freeze" their faces with Botox. We'll see how that pans out when they've had so many injections that their eyebrows are higher than The Joker's. Maybe I wouldn't have my elevens if I'd started Botox twenty years ago, but back then it was fairly new, and you'd hear horror stories about women not being able to close their eyes after getting injected. Or they'd end up looking like that Cat Woman who's everyone's cautionary tale. It was also more shameful than normal to get any work done on your face back then, where now it's as regular to some people as a tooth cleaning. But with or without cosmetic help, Jessica is gorgeous and lovely and brilliant, so I was happy to have her by my side for moral support and muscle, if needed.

After a minute or two, my name was called, and we followed a flawless medical assistant named Kayleigh (of course) into the exam room. Out of her earshot, Jessica leaned into me and whispered, "I'm not going to say anything unless I need to. I'll just sit in the corner with my expensive purse and look intimidating."

"You'd look more intimidating if you were actually able to frown," I whispered back.

"I take that as a compliment. Now be prepared to be upselled," she said.

Kayleigh took my vitals and had me sign some paperwork promising to not sue if the procedure disintegrated my face. Then Dr. White Man waltzed into the room like he was walking onto a yacht. If he'd had a scarf, it would have been apricot. "Now, what do we have here?" he said, completely disinterested in my middle-aged ass. I stammered, "Uh, elevens" and pointed at my face in shame. For a brief second, I hoped that he'd clutch his stethoscope and gasp, "What? You're gorgeous! Go home, kid. Come back in twenty years. There's nothing I, an arrogant dickhead doctor, can do to make you look any better than you already do! I am not *God*."

Instead, he gave me a fleeting glance, muttered, "Uh huh, uh huh, uh huh," then said to Kayleigh, "I think twenty units should do it," and she pulled out a needle and some vials of the good shit. I didn't know if twenty was a lot or a little, so I glanced over at Jessica who gave me a quick nod, like any good consigliere. The next thing I knew, the needle jammed into my forehead once, twice, three times, each with a creepy crunch sound as it went through my . . . forehead bone? . . . while Kayleigh whapped my shoulder to distract me from the pain. Dr. Man said, "Just a little pinch . . . and other pinch . . . and . . ." Then he abruptly stopped, and she dabbed me with a cotton ball while he mumbled something about how I should call the office if I came down with a bad reaction and/or death. "That's it?" I squeaked, with another look at Jessica, who I saw was now busy reading a brochure about CoolSculpting. "I'm done?"

"Yes," Dr. Man said, "except for the quote I'm giving you for blepharoplasty."

"What . . . what's blepharoplasty? Is it like blasphemy? Did I ask about that?"

"It's eyelid surgery. Your eyelids are droopy, and Botox won't fix that. Here, look at these pics. Kayleigh had hers done last year."

He then pulled out his iPhone and speedily showed me the Before picture of twenty-five-year-old Kayleigh's eyes and the After photo of twenty-five-year-old Kayleigh's eyes. She looked perfect in both of them. I honestly couldn't tell the difference— BECAUSE SHE'S TWENTY-FIVE. I was about to tell Dr. Man that he clearly doesn't know how Before and After ads are supposed to work, but then fresh-lidded Kayleigh popped up with a three-page printout in her hand that described my blepharoplasty procedure and the cost: five-thousand dollars. I gave Jessica a fraught glance, and she rolled her eyes and mouthed "upsell." Wasn't I supposed to leave this appointment feeling better and not worse? I thought insecure old lady handholding was included in the fee.

All done with Exam Room 3 Crone Patrol, Dr. Man patted my arm, said, "Just see the girls at the front desk to get it scheduled, thankyougoodluckbye," and zoomed off to crush the ego of the next sucker waiting. The entire experience took under ten minutes. I walked out of the room with Jessica, a bit dazed, paid my bill (three hundred dollars), and then we left the building and headed to the bright parking lot. "You look . . . good," she said half-heartedly with an appraisal of my forehead. "Not too red and bruised yet. A bit of dried blood, but it matches your lipstick."

"Thanks for the support," I answered woozily. "I think I feel a headache coming on for many, many reasons. That whole eyelid thing was random and disturbing, right?"

"Don't worry about it," she answered. "Next time he'll probably mention the labial folds around your mouth, then start working his way down. They all do that. Your eyelids aren't *that* bad for your age. I gotta go but send me a picture of your face in five to seven days when you're no longer able to scowl."

"They aren't *that* bad?" I replied in a hurt voice, but by then she was already halfway to her Tesla and my headache had gotten worse. Was the poison eating away at my frontal lobe? Was my head going to explode like a can of peas? What was in the waiver I signed, anyway? Did I need a living will?

Spoiler: I lived. And, as promised, in five to seven days I sent Jessica a selfie. In it, I looked pretty, happy, and most important, devoid of any face math. No more big number eleven on me. Not only had the Botox worked to smooth the creases between my eyebrows, but it also firmed up my forehead lines and made me appear more awake and less crabby. I once again looked like I sleep eight hours a night instead of driving a Dr Pepper semi-truck cross country. I hated to admit it, but Dr. Man knew what he was doing. Plus, I was pleased that I didn't completely lose my ability to move my muscles in that area, so I didn't look like a frozen doll or one of the weirder Real Housewives (Ramona). The pictures I saw of myself afterwards looked better too. My eye was no longer immediately drawn to the space between my eyebrows. That said, I'm still not 100 percent in love with Botox and what it is and what it represents, no matter how well it worked for me. But at this age, I guess anything it takes to help you feel better is good. Some of my friends like Botox and fillers, and some are completely repulsed by it, like my friend Laura. "Watch me try to frown," I told her once after an appointment, and she told me to stop because it made her upset.

"Okay," I told her. "Just know that *I'm* not upset. But if I ever am, you won't be able to tell on my face, so I'll hold up my middle finger instead." And then I had to apologize for being a jerk because I haven't quite perfected cosmetic procedure humor yet.

I've now had Botox at least four more times. Maybe five. I try to wait about six months between appointments, mostly because of the expense, and there wasn't much point to doing it during the pandemic when I could just wear a hat on Zoom calls. I like what it does for me, but I also know there are bigger priorities in my life than my face. Plus, there are now better Instagram filters so I can digitally scrub out my elevens in a pinch. I also haven't gone back to see Dr. Man and Kayleigh because I found another place that's more friendly and female-owned. It's in a strip mall and not a Mediterranean palace, but that's okay. So far, they haven't tried to upsell me on anything, even though I'm sure that if I mentioned "face lift" I'd have a quote in my hand and a hospital gown on my body in about two seconds flat.

It's tempting to not do any of this stuff, to just throw caution to the wind and let what happens happen. To truly not give a shit about aging. We've all seen that mom at school who lets her hair go gray at age thirty-five and only wears sack dresses and macaroni jewelry. She's aging gracefully and in a way that makes her happy, yet most of us grimace instead of applaud her for being authentic. Why is that? I'm pretty sure I'd much rather take her granola route instead of the injectables path I'm on, but I don't. Not yet. I know the day will come when it no longer makes a difference to use hair dye or wear Spanx or invest in a push-up bra. I know the day will come when I'm at last comfortable in my skin and just grateful to still be kicking.

Fight to stay younger looking? Or decide that it's all bullshit and use that money on a trip to Egypt? My take on that depends on the day. Today I'm Googling things like "fraxel laser" and "chin thread lift." But tomorrow, maybe I'll lean toward just being happy with my naturally aging face because that's what faces do, if you're lucky enough to age. Besides, bridges always need trolls.

How Middle-Aged Women Can Look Stunning in Cell Phone Photos

Ladies, if you don't want the expense and hassle of cosmetic procedures to look younger in real life or, more importantly, in photos, I have good news. Now, there are countless apps and filters available to take years off your digital face with just the touch of a button. In the past, only famous people like Cher, Liberace, and Spuds MacKenzie reaped the benefits of photo retouching, but now that magic is available to middle-aged wankers like you too. Wrinkles, woes, and worries, begone!

Here's how to look like a million bucks:

1. First, know where to pose when taking a group photo. If there are more than two people, insist that you're in the middle. You must never, ever get stuck in the end position, AKA The Fat Arm Spot. "Wow, when did her arm become a side of beef?" people will gasp when they see you on Facebook looking like a Green Bay Packer. I'll tell you when: when you let Janice take the middle position, dumbass.

2. If the photos are snapped on someone else's phone, immediately ask to see them so you can delete the ones you don't like. This may involve force. Think Sean Penn in the '80s.

3. If the photos are taken on your phone, relax and only save the pictures that are flattering to you. Trash the rest. It's okay to occasionally post the photos where you look good and your friends don't, but be careful. Revenge is a dish best served on Instagram.

4. There are many editing apps available for the iPhone, so pick one that's top rated. You may think a free app is fine, but you are wrong. Anyone over forty needs the latest and greatest MIT nerd technology. Besides, would you rather pay three

dollars for an app that erases your forehead lines or three hundred dollars for Botox that erases your forehead lines? The choice is simple, crêpey.

5. The best filters to make your face look more youthful have names like "Soft Focus," "Vaseline," and "Just Had Cataract Surgery." Stay away from any filter with a name like "Natural," "Aging Gracefully," or "God Thinks I'm Beautiful So I Don't Give a Shit If You Do."

6. If the filter isn't doing the trick, you may want to use a feature called "healing." This digital surgeon lets you erase lines, dark spots, and pimples from your face via swiping your finger on the screen. You can also erase entire people from the photo, and if they comment, "What happened to me?" just answer, "I think that's a question for your therapist, Dad."

7. Do not use so many filters that your nose and/or other facial features appear to be missing. You don't want to look like a specter from another dimension in the group selfie at Girls Wine & Painting Night. Nor do you want to look like you had plastic surgery in a veterinarian's office. A good rule of thumb is if you're holding a newborn baby in a photo and you look like the one who just came out of the womb, take off a filter or two.

8. Finally, when you're meeting someone in real life who has only seen your retouched and filtered photos online, be honest in advance. Come clean. Let them know that you're a middle-aged feminist, and you don't believe women should subject their faces to fillers, serums, and peels just to fit into an outdated patriarchal beauty standard. Women should be loved for who they are, not what they look like. Then dim the lights, put on your bee keeper's outfit, and take a new profile pic.

IT'S A SLIPPERY SLOPE

Thank you for coming into the office today! I've given your forehead a good look and recommend thirty units of Botox. I promise you'll look ten years younger and, more important, a lot less angry. What do you have to be angry about, anyway? You're a middle-aged woman in America.

The Botox smoothed away the credit card slot between your eyes, but we should do something about your eyelids now. The eyes are the window to the soul, and yours look like they're covered in discount curtains from HomeGoods. Read this pamphlet on blepharoplasty, then call my assistant, Jules, with questions. Jules is your age, but she refuses to look it.

Your eyelids healed nicely, but now I'm noticing your big cheeks. Want me to suck a little fat out? It's a simple procedure. Jules, set up time for ol' Satchmo here. Haha, just a little jazz age joke about your face, why are you so offended?

The cheeks are looking nice and emaciated now, almost street urchin level, but here's a question: how attached are you to your ears? "Very"? Okay, let's move on to your turkey neck.

I know those months of Fraxel/CO2/Collagen Induction therapy weren't fun, but it really did wonders for your *décolletage*. That's a French word meaning "upper chesticle area." But unfortunately, now my eye is drawn to your saggy breasts. Take a look, Jules. This is what happened to women who did high-impact aerobics before the sports bra was invented. Yikes. How many kids did you nurse? A six-pack?

Hmm, I thought the new C-cups would help your stomach and love handles not seem so sizable, but I guess I thought wrong. Now your torso looks like a Swiss mountain range. Riiiiiiii-cola! Haha. Well, no need to fret because we now offer bulk liposuction financing.

Hey, are you in our Ugly Ass Middle-Ager rewards program? Get her signed up, Jules.

I'm sorry to tell you this, but I've done pretty much everything I can from head to toe, and you still look like a woman over forty. We're probably out of options unless you'd like to try this new procedure we have. It's not FDA-approved, but it probably will be now that our government has just given up completely because people are injecting horse dewormer into their bodies instead of getting a vaccine. It's the Wild West! Anyway, just lie down on the table and relax, and our proprietary laser will zap across your body and render it invisible to the human gaze. Sorry, but it's the only option you have left. Jules, hand me my goggles.

CHAPTER TEN

I'M WEARING A BIGGER SIZE NOW

I became squishy around age forty-seven. My stomach region, an area I would have never described as "taut" but still fairly contained, suddenly exploded like it was a tube of Pillsbury crescent rolls that someone pressed with a soup spoon. KAPOW! I was wider too. "That's the famous middle-age spread," my way-too-honest friend Stacy said with a poke to my belly when I lifted up my shirt to show her. "It's doughboy time." Then, when I looked understandably upset, "Sorry. Dough*woman*. Calm down, feminazi."

I didn't believe her. A lifetime of being a woman in America had conditioned me to believe that any weight gain is entirely my fault, so the new squishiness couldn't be due to my age or my hormones. That was ridiculous. It obviously happened because I was weak and lazy and a piece of shit. Clearly, I'd overdone it on queso and margaritas again, which is easy and enjoyable to do. In Austin, we don't meet for coffee, we meet for tequila and tacos. For that reason, I was no stranger to needing to lose a little flab from time to time. This newfound stomach problem was an easy fix, I thought. I'd get back on track by just eating less and exercising more like I'd done a million times. No need to panic and buy bigger pants with elastic waistbands. No need for a cabbage soup crash diet or prescription speed or whatever it is that poor wild-eyed floozy Marie Osmond desperately hawks every January. Belly Fat Elimination plan in place, I marched into the grocery store and bought forty dollars of fruit and vegetables that I swore this time I'd eat before they rotted in the vegetable crisper where we keep our cans of hard seltzer. Then I sprawled on the couch, balanced my iPhone on a bowl of tortilla chips, and downloaded the Weight Watchers app. I knew I'd be tankini ready in no time.

Now, if you're a blessed creature who's never tried Weight Watchers, know that unlike the old plans I did in the '80s and '90s that restricted dieters to certain food, the new plan lets you eat whatever you want. Each food has its own number of points and you're given a total amount every day to adhere to. You could wisely eat a couple points here and a couple points there and load up on vegetables that count as zero points, or you could just say "fuck it, life's too short" and go balls to the wall and blow your entire thirty-point daily limit on a single Big Mac. That's what we in Weight Watchers Nation call "legend status."

Some people struggle with the plan's restrictions, but I do well with this type of controlled freedom. I'm a person who'll stay up until 3 a.m. bingeing a *Reno 911!* marathon, so it's nice to have some limitations. Plus, it was kind of fun to track everything I ate on the WW app, like I was playing *Angry Chubby Birds* or something. Before long, I knew how many points a cracker was versus how many points a bigger cracker was. I ate the type of bread that has the fewest points (carbs are allowed on Oprah's "I love breadddddd!" WW). I counted each almond I ate, drank oceans of water, and either worked out or went for long walks every day. Sometimes I walked with my dog Teddy, who desperately needs to lose weight per his veterinarian but that's his personal journey and I refuse to body-shame a poodle. It can't be easy to have the neighborhood nickname of "El Gordito."

Everything I did for two weeks on WW was to make myself healthier and thinner. Well, let's be honest—thinner. I didn't care so much about the healthy part because I was being stupid and shallow. Everything I did also made me a hungry bitch with sore knees, but that was okay because I knew I was on my way back to my usual shape and size. "Nothing tastes as good as skinny feels," I whispered to Teddy one night while we both stared raptly at a Pizza Hut commercial. "Not even that lizard in the backyard that's looking more and more like a three-point snack option we'll probably fight over soon." Finally, after fourteen days of tracking and walking and depriving myself of any type of enjoyment besides a six-point glass of chardonnay every night, I stepped on the scale, eager to see the diminished number. I knew I'd lost *at least* five pounds. Nope.

I'd gained five fucking pounds.

"It's your metabolism, dummy," my way-too-honest friend Stacy told me when I called her to cry about it. "I told you that before. It slows down as you get older. Like, a lot. All you can do now is figure out how to boost your metabolism because that's the only way to get rid of your muffin top. Well, besides liposuction, but you have college and retirement to save for so you probably can't afford it."

That conversation taught me three things: 1) I had a metabolism, 2) I had a muffin top, and 3) I probably shouldn't rely on Stacy for any pep talks going forward.

But I took her advice and made an appointment with my primary care physician, Google.com, to see what I should do about it. The articles I read reminded me that "metabolism" is the process by which a human body converts what it eats and drinks into energy. And, much like a woman's willingness to be nice and friendly to men, it slows to a crawl as you get older. Your body burns fewer calories in middle age, so the calories that once put a spring in your step now put a fat in your ass. It's this slowed metabolism, plus a typically more sedentary lifestyle in your forty-plus years (see: bingeing *Reno 911!*) that leads to what medical experts and hack humor writers call "Couch Potato Syndrome." A name that both insults me and makes me hungry for butter, so I am obviously afflicted with it.

The reasons for a slowed metabolism in women are biological and, like most depressing things in middle age, the fault of our hormones. My B- in high school science class doesn't give me the skills to explain it much better than this, but I think what happens is our bodies change once we're no longer able (or willing) to reproduce. The same reason we become invisible at a certain age. This no doubt started back in prehistoric times when middle-aged cavewomen became old (which in those days was maybe twenty?) and gray and tired of taking any more shit from the men in the tribe. The cavemen then called them stuck-up skanks and kicked them out of the cave, much like I'd be booted out of a fraternity party if I sashayed in and said, "'Sup, dickweeds? Me and my Spanx are here to drain your keg and mock your grades." (Which I'd totally like to do if you know of any upcoming ragers.)

But here's the important part of the story: Once those cavewomen were rejected by the cavemen and pushed into the wild, they had no other choice but to grow stores of fat to stay alive. The ice age version of a chunky sweater from Nordstrom. Therefore, the continuation of the human race basically depends on older women getting flabby and repelling men into the arms of firm younger women with fresh eggs. It makes sense. Of course, there's a 100 percent likelihood that none of what I just said is true, but I hope there's an anthropologist out there who's documented an ancient cave painting depicting an angry woman with love handles and thunder thighs wrestling a saber-toothed tiger to the death.

All of that is to say that evolution is why I can't fit into my pants.

If you're over the age of forty-five, none of what I just said is a surprise. There's no way you gasped and said, "Women's bodies change in midlife?" Every single middle-aged woman I know claims that the diet and exercise plan they've always followed, the one that usually, or mostly, kept them in shape, no longer works once they hit their mid-forties. "How could I gain five pounds overnight? All I had to eat yesterday was a Tic Tac," my friend Amanda once whined to me. "Should I only have half a Tic Tac? Or do I need to cut out Tic Tacs entirely? How much sugar does plain fucking air have? IS THAT TOO MUCH TO ASK?" No matter where I am or who I'm with, all I have to say is, "I can't stop gaining weight," and within seconds I'm surrounded by sweaty, desperate women telling me how many calories are in a tater tot. I've had the squishy stomach convo with women in airports, in clothing stores, and while waiting in line at the grocery store with a cart full of Pringles and ham slices because it's my cheat day. Once I was at the library and fell into a conversation about books with the friendly same-aged stranger standing next to me in the fiction section. We'd just discussed why we were sick of thrillers with "Girl" in the title when she suddenly grabbed the flat tire around her waist with both hands and whispered, *I call her Hortense the Destroyer.* I am not making that up. I didn't know what to do at the time besides slowly back away to the safety of the reference desk, but now I kind of wish I'd gotten her number so she could text me updates. I'd love to hear details about the havoc Hortense is wreaking around town.

"Millennial Brunch Sabotaged by Middle-Aged Love Handle."

"Tragedy at Soul Cycle When Out of Control Menopot Crushes Instructor."

"'Pinch This Inch, Assholes!' Woman Screams After Destroying an Everything but Water Swimsuit Store in Fit of Rage and Hunger."

There's a saying that goes, "There are no strangers here, only friends who haven't met." In midlife it's more, "There are no strangers here, only women bonding over why the fuck they now have back fat."

As I said, it was fairly easy for me to get in shape back when I had a working metabolism, those halcyon days of my twenties and thirties. Not as easy as a male getting in shape, of course. All a man has to do to lose ten pounds is skip a meal and take a small flight of stairs. Maybe switch to light beer for a night. "No, thanks, hon, I'll pass on the second dessert because I'm in training for a marathon." But in the past, if I wanted to lose a few pounds, like for a beach vacation or a class reunion or to sweet-talk my way out of a fine at traffic court, I'd just ramp up my workout schedule. I'd cut out all sweets and snacks for a week or two, and it almost always worked because my body was still young and supple and my pelvis needed to be biologically attractive for the survival of the human race. One week when I was in my twenties, I worked out three times and actually looked into entering a bodybuilding competition because of the new muscles that popped up. "Yeah, don't do that," Chris said. "For many, many reasons."

It wasn't until my mid-thirties that my body really changed, and that was mostly because I was pregnant with Sam at thirty-four and Jack at thirty-six. I thought that growing a human meant I could eat whatever I wanted to eat, so I gained sixty pounds with Sam. "I'm eating for two," I'd announce while eating enough pizza for an entire baseball team's end-of-the-season trophy party. I weighed the most I ever have in my life—and hopefully will ever weigh because it didn't look good on me. One day I put on a jean jacket that no longer fit around my huge stomach and my dear husband thought it was funny to call me Chris Farley. "You'd better watch out or you're going to be living *in a van down by the river*! Haha!" It was not funny, and it still comes up in fights twenty years later. My competitive eating streak finally stopped when my kind OB/GYN gently said, "You may want to cut down on the second helpings if possible. Pregnancy isn't a free-for-all, you know."

But even after I had the babies, my metabolism still chugged along nicely. The combination of nursing, walking, and new motherhood stress got me back to my pre-baby weight fairly quickly. By "pre-baby," I don't mean I was like one of those awful "Bikini After Baby!" photo spreads in *Us Weekly*—the ones that show some variety of Kardashian two hours after giving birth, standup paddle boarding in Malibu while her placenta floats beside her like a deranged otter. I didn't look *that* amazing, but I didn't have to run out and buy a bunch of new pants, either.

It's not at all lost on me how good I had it then, and how good I had it for the first forty years of my life. I know that I'm lucky I don't have any underlying health or other issues that make it difficult to lose weight, like many women do. Attaining results from just diet and exercise isn't a thing to be taken lightly, and I'm fortunate that I've always felt like I've had a modicum of control over my body via my genetics. That doesn't mean I haven't spent most of my life fretting about my weight, however. Of course I have. What woman raised in America hasn't compared her body to other women's? From the age of thirteen on I worried about my size. A lot. Was my body thin enough? Was it hot enough? Was it enough like the bodies the boys all drooled over? Like the naked seventeen-year-old girl that takes a shower in *Sixteen Candles*? (Which is so, so inappropriate when viewed as an adult, John Hughes.) The insecurity took up way too much of my life.

There are many reasons for not seeing my body as it really was, of course, but I attribute a lot of my low self-esteem to being a proud member of Gen X. If you grew up in the '80s, you know there was no such thing as body positivity. We had none of the great "love your size!" or "all bodies are perfect" messaging that's out now. We never saw a swimsuit model over size two or a not model-thin woman in an MTV video. "She's got legs, and she knows how to use 'em—and they're size fourteen!" Nope. There certainly wasn't anyone like Lizzo back then, or even anyone famous above size ten who wasn't the butt of jokes. Nobody batted an eye when they heard words like "gigantic" and "obese" and other insults that no longer fly, and shouldn't have ever flown, when describing a person of size. I was called a "fat ass" in junior high more than once, and I don't think I weighed over one-hundred-thirty pounds at the time. I'm finally over it, I think, but I do kind of wish I could go back to those years and feel as comfortable with my shape as a lot of the younger generation is now. They'll proudly wear a crop top no matter what their size, and if you don't like it, that's your damn problem. It's wonderful.

After I didn't lose much weight at all in my six weeks of Weight Watchers, I took Stacy's advice and tried to find a way to boost my middle-aged metabolism. There's no shortage of articles and websites claiming to know how to "lose belly fat in 10 days!" Some of the suggested methods I found seemed sensible, like "drink a smoothie for breakfast" and "take probiotics." Other suggested methods to fire up the metabolism were a bit more looney tunes. (Hello, Dr. Oz.) One website advised eating a bunch of chili peppers to really "rev your system." Uh, no. Not going to do that. I'm from North Dakota and think ketchup is spicy. Another idea I found that seemed reasonable was to "start your day with hot lemon water," but who really wants to drink hot lemon water? Maybe if there's a shot of Tito's vodka in it, but that's usually not a good idea in the morning unless you're on vacation with your children. Plus, how can something as tame as water with a dash of citrus actually combat the violent forces attacking my southern border? I need heavier artillery than *that*.

I finally found some sane advice on metabolism boosting and it's this: get more active. Unfortunately, just walking, even the fast walking that makes you look like a moron rushing to a bathroom because she needs to poop, isn't intense enough. To really make a difference, you have to do something that elevates your heart rate for at least twenty minutes. Normally that'd be fine because I've always liked cardio, but jumping around like Jamie Lee Curtis in *Perfect* isn't too appealing to me anymore due to both the knee issue and the pee issue. I discovered the latter during a mini trampoline class that was actually paused midway through so all of the middle-aged moms in the class could take a potty break. But when I looked at my workout options, I realized that there aren't many choices between high intensity workouts and silver sneakers stretching classes. And, since so far nobody's trademarked a Midlife Wanker Workout, I decided to start with the high intensity ones. Even if that meant that I was now the "old lady" in the back of the class who looked destined to be the first in line to take the gym's new defibrillator out for a spin.

The Gen Z/millennial workouts I tried to boost my metabolism included: indoor rhythm cycling (which sounds like something a cult would call their method of birth control), indoor rock climbing, early morning boot camp, and a few of those stupid barre classes where you basically just squeeze your glutes and stare at yourself in the mirror for sixty straight minutes. But while each of those activities came with their own challenges, rhythm cycling was by far the worst.

My friend Nicole and I had gone to regular spin class for years, so we thought the shiny new rhythm cycling studio that opened in our neighborhood would be the same thing. Nope. The whole place was stark white with low neon lighting, like the set of a stylistic horror movie about serial killers of the future. As soon as we walked in, the vibrating front desk staff yelled, "Are you here to get PUMPED?"

and I didn't know how to answer that. "Yes? I mean, I guess? I'll try? STOP STARING AT ME, I AM NOT AN ANIMAL." Every instructor was a twenty-five-year-old cool kid, and they blasted hardcore rap songs with explicit lyrics that we were supposed to move our bodies to somehow. While holding two-pound weights. Trust me when I say that rhythm cycling to music that has no rhythm is a strange thing indeed. Maybe you know how, but I sure don't. I know how to move to Cameo and Prince. Crank up some Wang Chung and I'll pedal along happily. But the music—plus the hipsters on their teacher bikes screaming what they thought were inspirational things at us like, "Pump dat damn ass!" and "Fuck yeah, bitches!"—made it a fairly hostile environment to find yourself in at 1 p.m. on a Tuesday.

"Why do I feel like we're in a Soviet work camp?!" a sweaty Nicole screamed at me one day after a male instructor named Merlin ran up to her bike and shouted, "Werk werk werk it, slut! Yass queen!"

"I DON'T KNOW, BUT I WANT OUT," I huffed back. "I HATE IT HERE." It wasn't your mother's Jazzercise, that's for fucking sure.

The last rhythm cycling class I attended, the one where I was by far the oldest person in the room and also the only person not wearing lash extensions for a workout, was by far the worst one. The pierced-everywhere ride instructor with an ironic Bart Simpson leg tattoo dimmed the lights, blasted Rihanna, then got off her bike and scurried around the room shrieking, "Do it, warriors! You're all warriors! LET ME HEAR YOU, YOU FUCKING WARRIORS!" Everybody in the class enthusiastically pedaled faster and whooped back at her but not me. I immediately stopped pedaling and said, "*Warriors?* Look around, Kassidy! We're not villagers fighting off Hezbollah, we're ten suburban women and a man bun stupid enough to pay twenty-five dollars to pedal in place for an hour!" I'm sure it would have really stung and made her reconsider her whole approach if she'd been able to hear me over the whoops from the rest of the class and the thumpa-thumpa from the speakers. I miss the good old days of doing the grapevine to Captain & Tennille in the community center.

My quest to find a class that would boost my metabolism and not make me want to kill everyone else in the room finally took me to the unavoidable, ubiquitous Orange Theory, the workout chain that's grown like crazy over the past few years. You can't swing a vintage legwarmer in the suburbs without hitting an Orange Theory. But I like it, it works, and so far, it hasn't made me feel homicidal. I've now been a member for over four years, and I plan to keep going until I actually do need the gym's defibrillator. The sixty-minute classes are half cardio and half weights, which is a great combo for calorie burning/ metabolism boosting, as well as for bone density. Yep, bone density. Yet another thing to worry about because *we aren't dealing with enough.*

Orange Theory's big claim is that you'll continue to burn fat the next day after a class, so it therefore increases your metabolism more than most workouts. I'm not entirely sure if that's true, but it seems to have stopped my midsection from spreading as fast as it was before. Chernobyl has finally been contained. The radioactive cloud can fit into her swim skirt again. The best part about it, though, is that I usually attend classes with my friends Amanda and the aforementioned straight shooter Stacy. We call ourselves The Sweaty Wrecking Crew because we're like the girls that get in trouble for having bad attitudes in PE class. For example:

1. We loudly groan, "Oh, fuckkkkkkk no" whenever the instructor says the class will include jumping.
2. Stacy will sometimes add, "That's not good for women who've had a baby, you know! Things are not ideal down there!"
3. Amanda often eats when she's on the treadmill.

4. Instead of trying to look cute for our workouts like the younger women, we often wear oversized elementary school carnival t-shirts.

5. If we don't want to do push-ups, we . . . don't do push-ups.

Even though we're usually the oldest in class, besides the seventy-five-year-old men there on doctor's orders, none of us ever feel embarrassed or out of place. We have each other, but we're also past the point of caring if we're as thin or as fit as anyone else in the class. We don't compare ourselves to anyone anymore, and it feels great. The class is really welcoming, too, despite our sometimes obnoxious Gen-X vigilantism. One day, a nice twenty-something instructor named Anthony yelled, "Whooo! Springsteen!" when a Bryan Adams song came on the speakers and the three of us burned about two-hundred calories each by rushing to the front desk to report him after the class was over. I almost sprained an ankle in my haste.

"What the hell, did y'all tattle on me?"

"Yes, and we'd do it again. Don't ever fuck around with Springsteen."

I'd like to say that at this point in my life, I've almost accepted that my body isn't the same as it was in my thirties, or even my forties. Much like the ice caps melting, the middle-age spread has happened, and it will continue to happen, and the reality cannot be denied. But I've made peace with it because what choice do I have? Why drive myself crazy with diets and extreme workouts or even surgery to fit some ideal that I don't even care about anymore? My body is healthy and strong, and I don't take that for granted. I never should have taken it for granted, but I was too stupid to realize that back in my Slimfast-seems-like-a-great-idea! days. I deeply appreciate my ability to move around without any issues, and my ability to take a walk with Teddy and keep up with him unless he sees a squirrel that needs attacking.

It feels good to have shifted my thinking from "I have to work out" to "I get to work out." It feels good to know what food my body likes. Would I love to have a tauter tummy and smaller pants? Of course, I would. I'm not that evolved yet. It takes work. Still, if I'm ever pushed out of the cave and have to fend for myself, I think I'll do just fine. I'm a fucking warrior.

Nine Ways I Wish I Could Boost My Metabolism

1. Rolling my eyes when I hear the twenty-year-old woman in the dressing room next to me say she's "Like, so fat" because her regular size-two bikini doesn't fit while I'm busy sobbing into a swim skirt I once saw a senior citizen wear on a Carnival Cruise.

2. Knocking on the twenty-year-old woman's dressing room to tell her to stop worrying about her shape because she's beautiful no matter what, then trying to take my own advice when purchasing the swim skirt.

3. An '80s movie cop breakfast of doughnuts, bacon, and candy. And a swig of whiskey while I cough up a lung and mutter, "I'm too old for this shit."

4. Pushing my cart that's filled with Doritos and boxes of Miss Clairol gray root touch-up through the grocery store while the sound system blasts Madonna songs I partied to in high school.

5. Grudges.

6. Sticking a 10K sticker on my car even though I've never run a 10K, and I'm not exactly sure how far 10K is because the metric system never really took off in America, but I think 10K is ten-thousand miles?

7. Binge-watching cooking shows and yelling at the contestants for doing it wrong even though I've broken our oven twice when making frozen pizza.

8. Writing a movie about living in a far-off land where I'm considered frail, and the townspeople make it their mission to plump me up with bread, cheese, and big bottles of wine that never give you a headache or make you drunk-dial your nemesis from the gym. Wait, that place might actually exist and it might be called "Italy."

9. Probably more grudges.

CHAPTER ELEVEN

I'M WEARING THE NAME MA'AM NOW

No word in the English language makes a woman feel older than the word "ma'am." Well, maybe "Crazy Old Bat," but that's three words. We all start off life as the cute-sounding "girl," then move on to "young woman," then "Miss," "Ms.," or "Mrs.," then maybe a few years of "bitch," only not in the fun way that millennials call each other "bitch," more like the pejorative way Gen X does. We oldies want it to sting. "That's the last time you sleep with my husband! Enjoy being stabbed with this fourteen-carat gold letter opener, bitch!" (We watched a lot of *Dynasty* at an impressionable age.) But ultimately, all women no matter who they are will one day reach the humbling milestone of being called "ma'am." Sorry, that's just how it is. I don't make the insulting name rules.

My "ma'aming" happened a little earlier than it would have in other parts of the world because I live in Texas. Probably the only time in history that the Lone Star State has been progressive. But "ma'am" is prevalent here because it's a staple of polite cowboy lexicon. I know this to be true because I hear it a lot when I visit my parents in Nevada. They spend most of their retiree free time watching old Westerns on cable. Sometimes they'll watch a Western more than once because they don't remember that they've seen it before. "It's not like there's a big difference in any of them," my dad says. "It's mostly a lot of horses and rocks." But every time I'm at their house, we get our snacks, stretch out on their reclining couch that's like what I imagine a seat on a private jet is like, and enjoy movies like *Rio Grande* and *Ride the High Country* and *Cheyenne Autumn*. In almost every one of these movies, a gunslinger will tip his hat and drawl, "Afternoon, ma'am," to any townswoman who isn't a prostitute. Then a few minutes later, the well-mannered gunslinger who was just so polite with his "ma'am" meets an overly dramatic end in an exciting pistol duel. We usually make it through one and a half of these movies before my mom finally snaps and says, "For crissakes, stop flailing around and just die, Pecos. I want to switch to *Dateline* now. Let's see what bad things the youth pastors did this week." I don't live in an old-timey Western, so nobody's ever fallen off a saloon balcony after calling me "ma'am," but I wouldn't be terribly upset if they did. Not even if they fell on a loose spur.

My first ma'aming is snugly lodged into my memory like a codependent tick. We all know insults have more staying power in our brains than compliments. I remember every single mean thing ever said to me in junior high, but did any invited guests say I looked good on my wedding day? Maybe Gus the caterer did, but I can't recall. I'm sure my husband, Chris, gave me praise of some sort, but that's probably because he felt obligated, being the groom and all. It's in the marriage contract, I think. "Love, honor, say 'wow you look really hot'!" Anyway, it's a shame that the space in my brain where that compliment should be is instead taken up by the memory of Jerry Reynolds calling me Girl Sasquatch in seventh-grade math class. I'm pretty sure Jerry is a youth pastor now. Maybe my mom's seen him on *Dateline*.

Back to The Incident.

I was only in my late thirties that day. Still an unwrinkled innocent baby not yet beaten down by life. I didn't even know what a tunic *was* back then. If memory serves, I was feeling cute and energetic when I sashayed into the Starbucks near my house. Unlike now when I basically slide into local places like a slick European spy, hoping nobody from school sees me because I don't want to hear yet another recap of how I disappointed them as Room Mom in 2007. But that day I bounced up to the counter and smiled at the attractive guy barista, who didn't seem much older than me, and cheerfully gave him my order.

(Note: the reason I smiled isn't because I'm a flirty person. I'm the opposite of flirty. Nirty? I basically freeze like an introverted fish whenever someone of the opposite sex tries to talk me up. Once, when I was in my twenties and working at Warner Bros., a semi-famous actor leaned on my desk and purred, "If you have some free time later tonight, maybe you could give me a tour of the studio lot." And, rather than saying something like, "I could give you a tour of many exciting places, lover," with a sly grin, I blinked at him like someone who'd just escaped an underground compound and said, "Why? Don't you have a map? Can you ask Leonard the golf cart mechanic to help you?" That social ineptitude is the reason I'm not living in a Bel Air mansion with an Emmy winner right now.)

I was friendly to the coffee guy that day, and I even offered up a bit of chitchat, like we were established neighborhood buddies who see each other on the regular. I often strike up conversations with store people to be nice, but also because it sometimes leads to free things, like the time I had a nineteen-dollar car wash comped because I told the cashier she looked just like Ginger Spice. Alas, that day at Starbucks, my charm offensive didn't get me anything but insulted. Right after I said the original line, "Pretty slow in here today, compared to the usual," came the bitch slap heard 'round the coffee shop.

"Anything else I can get for you today, ma'am?"

". . ."

"Ma'am?"

"Uhhh, just give me whatever cookie has the most frosting because I'm obviously close to dying of elderly decrepitude. How much do I owe you for the bucket of cold water you just poured all over my ego, *sir*?"

Wham, bam, I was motherfucking ma'amed.

I know I sound overly sensitive about it, but that's only because I am overly sensitive about it. And while the first ma'am hurts, so does the hundredth ma'am. Probably the thousandth too, which I'm fast approaching. To me, and to many other women my age, "ma'am" isn't just a simple word. Rather, it's a hard dose of reality. A push down the stairs of life that ends in a crying jag and an order of Amazon Prime tennis balls to put on the feet of your aluminum walker. "Ma'am" is a word that tells me that other people consider me old, even though that's not how I think of myself at all. It's a big divergence in perception. It's like if someone yelled, "Hey, brown-haired woman!" at me when I know full well that I'm a blonde. (The reason I know this is not only because I'm of Norwegian descent but also because my hair always matches my glass of chardonnay.) That said, hair color is a lot more straightforward than age, so if someone thinks I'm "ma'am" age, are they right or am I right in thinking that I'm not? Unfortunately, there's no way to control other people's individual ideas of when "ma'am" is appropriate. To quote the famous Bob Mankoff cartoon, "How about never—Is never good for you?"

My friend Cassie, who lives in New York City and who's just a year younger than me, was only recently ma'amed for the first time. She made it until almost fifty before the ma'am bomb was dropped on her like a tub full of expired Tab. Lucky duck. Unfortunately, it was dropped enough times by the teenage grocery sacker to make her a little weepy. "Would you like paper or plastic, ma'am? Bread on the top, ma'am? Oh, this is my favorite ice cream too, ma'am! Do you need me to help carry this bag out to your stagecoach, ma'am? Big night at the saloon, ma'am?" But how could she be upset with him because the poor kid probably thought he was being super polite. He didn't know he was giving an innocent customer an identity crisis that would haunt her for months. I empathized, but I admit that I was kind of jealous too. She managed to go a full decade longer than I did without experiencing a damn ma'am, mostly because she doesn't live in the South. It almost made moving to Brooklyn and paying four-thousand dollars a month for a cockroach-infested studio apartment enticing.

Cassie said the whole episode made her feel like "mutton dressed like ma'am," a brilliant description of feeling that you're young and a Miss, even though your wrinkles and Land's End all-purpose utility pants tell everyone else a different story. Baaaa.

Men don't face this "you're so old that we're calling you a new word now" indignity. Why would they? They're men. All men around the world are respectfully addressed as "Sir," or their language's equivalent, starting from a young age. And it continues until they die. I've even heard people address my sons as "Sir" throughout their lives, which is a ridiculous thing to say to a kid who probably had his WWE underwear on backwards at the time. I mean, I guess it's better than "young master" like you sometimes hear in British and *Star Wars* movies, but not by much.

Queen of Everything Beyoncé actually named one of her twins "Sir," which seems redundant because that kid will be called Sir his entire life anyway. Much like the centuries-old wedding terminology that names men the heroic "Best Men" and women the service-oriented "Maids of Honor," the prevalence of "sir" is yet another example of men receiving a baseline level of respect that women don't. Blech. Maybe we should start referring to any man over forty as "Pops" or "Gramps." Let's see how they like being minimized because they're older. "Paper or plastic today, Captain Saggy Balls?"

But while I don't enjoy "ma'am" in the least, I admit that I've now been called it for so long that it feels weird when people don't say it. In fact, it's almost more jarring when people address me as "Miss." When the "Miss" happens, I don't feel flattered or fooled. I certainly don't smile at the person saying it, like they just gave me a compliment. Rather, I narrow my eyes and purse my lips because I'm pretty sure they called me "Miss" to be cute, or, more often than not, they're a condescending asshole. Stay with me here: It's probably clear to both of us in the conversation that I'm no longer a "Miss," mostly because the two lines I sometimes have between my eyebrows are so deeply furrowed that the Jamaican bobsled team could use it as a racetrack, so why use it when "ma'am" is obviously a more appropriate word? Unless it's just to fuck with me?

I'm well aware that I'm a neurotic pain in the ass, thanks for asking.

Way worse than being called "Miss" in middle age is being called "young lady" or "girl" by someone younger. That's *definitely* condescending, no question about it. "Sorry to interrupt, but would you young ladies like another glass of wine? You went through that first round pretty fast!" Yes, *Josh*, we *would* like another glass and then many more glasses. Of course, I realize that Josh, like most younger waiters and bartenders, doesn't know to use my preferred term "Women That Are Superior to Me in All Ways" when addressing me and my peers, especially not here in the millennial kingdom of Austin, but come on. It's not necessary to stick "young" in front of "ladies." It just isn't. That's both pandering and gross. Do you think Josh would ever approach a table of dudes and say, "Would you young men like another glass of wine?" or "Anything yummy for you to nibble on tonight, boys? Any of you little lads feel like being *bad* and getting dessert?" No fucking way would Josh do that. They'd rip off his ironic mustache, then shove it into his mouth and high-five each other and grunt for the next two hours. The best thing for Josh to do to keep his tips up is just call everyone "folks" or "folx" no matter their gender or age.

I know I'm making a big deal out of being called "ma'am," as well as making a big deal out of not being called "ma'am," and I also know that's unreasonable. But the words people use to address me is something I've been grappling with for years because it feels like I've been stuck in a weird in-between age forever. I'm not young, but I'm also not *that* old. Or maybe I am that old and I just don't want to admit it. Girl, Miss, Mrs., Ms., Ma'am—which one fits me best? I don't know. Madame, like the French? That's not bad. I kind of like that. Even better, maybe it's best if we finally banish titles like "Sir," "Ma'am," and the like altogether. That seems to be where society is headed with younger generations rejecting the strict gender binary anyway, and it makes a whole lot of sense when you think about it. Why should gender and age come into play and lead you into an existential depression when all you're trying to do is just buy a fucking pack of gum at CVS? "Is that all for you today, ma'am?" YES, IT IS, HUMAN.

Eventually every woman will be called "ma'am," at least until our language and society move past these musty old distinctions and I don't foresee that happening in my lifetime. There will be no, as my friend Nancy puts it, Silence of the Ma'ams. A whole bunch of Americans only recently realized that calling a football team a racial slur isn't a great idea. So for now at least, we can't escape "ma'am" no matter how well we're aging or how youthful we think and act. Put on a tube top and a pair of booty shorts and start twerking like a twenty-year-old, and you'll still probably have someone say, "Ma'am, please stop causing a scene. Applebee's is a family establishment." Mutton dressed like lamb or mutton dressed like ma'am—we can't win.

I admit there's one word I don't mind being called as a form of address, and it's courtesy of Julio, our landscaper for the past fifteen years. Julio is possibly the worst landscaper on the planet because he doesn't seem to realize that we want our grass kept alive. I don't know how he manages to run a landscaping company despite not knowing the difference between a weed and a flower, but he does.

"You like these yellow roses I planted?"

"Those are dandelions, Julio."

"Okay, I'm gonna charge you fifty dollars for these yellow roses I planted."

But, he's cheap and reliable and a nice guy, so we keep working with him. He also refers to me by a word nobody else has in my entire life. It's kind of confusing, but I love it. "You want the trees trimmed, man?" he'll say. "Hey, man, what you want me to do with the leaves in the backyard? Blow them into your neighbor's yard again? They always come back, though. I don't know how that happens, man." Once, early on, I said, "Julio, why do you call me that? I'm not a man. You need to stop calling me that. It doesn't even make sense."

"You got it, man," he replied, "I won't do it anymore. Thanks, man." Then he swung his weed trimmer over to my canna lilies and cut off all the blooms.

Still, I started to like being called man. I got used to it. He wasn't judging me on my age or my looks or my gender, despite the word, which felt kind of freeing. Should we start calling other ma'am aged women "man"? Maybe they'd like it too.

But now that I think more about it, maybe Julio hasn't actually been saying "man" to me all these years, after all. Maybe that's just how I've heard it because he kind of mutters everything and he's got a '60s burnout vibe going on. Picture an old hippie with a Texas twang and at least ten cactus needles stuck in his backside most of the time. It's also super hard to hear him over the roar of the riding lawnmower he's usually on while I'm jogging after him, yelling, "Don't run over the dog!" Wait. Oh, shit. Has he been calling me "ma'am" and not "man" all of these years?

Wham, bam, it happened again.

CHAPTER TWELVE

I'M WEARING COOLING CLOTHS NOW

You can't really write about age and women and aged women without addressing the M word. It's the annoying, inevitable, bifocal-wearing elephant in the room that nobody really likes to talk about. Well, besides the people in the hit musical about it that features the horrifying parody disco song "Stayin' Awake/Night Sweatin'," that I don't ever plan on attending because I'm worried I'll go broke buying souvenir t-shirts. So let's talk about Menopause, baby.

Here's what I know: Menopause and its younger sister perimenopause are what happens when women get older and our reproductive systems start to slow and eventually shut down completely. Before I continue, here's a fun fact: I've mistakenly spelled "perimenopause" like "periomenopause" so many times that I now want to pitch the Oxygen network a gritty drama about a middle-aged Irish woman named Peri O'Menopause who lives in the countryside and avenges murders. She's super happy until she turns forty-five, and then she gets really agitated at all the unsolved crimes in her small county (what *is* it about those quaint country villages and all the murders?), flies into a hormonal rage, and, fortified with lots of Guinness and armed with a knitting needle, goes after all the predators in the area. Yes, it's an ageist, sexist, and culturally insensitive idea, but just think of all the merchandising possibilities and product tie-ins!

Per my internet research, most females are born with a finite number of eggs that are stored in the dairy case of our ovaries, and when they're all gone, menstruation ceases and we're officially in menopause. A Chico's credit card arrives in the mail the very next day. That all seems natural and normal and a positive thing if you're sick of buying tampons and dealing with period pain every month, and also if you're not having or done having children. But because nothing is easy, it's not quite that simple. The entire menopausal process can take years before you're finally free. *Years.* It's not exactly a walk in the park in a long, beige cardigan, either. Progesterone and estrogen levels fluctuate or may suddenly drop, and that can cause a whole host of unpleasant symptoms that I'll get into in a bit.

There are plenty of available resources and self-proclaimed experts on perimenopause and menopause, like my local Women's Hormonal Clinic that advertises on our morning news and features women who rave about their increased sex drive at 7 a.m., but both conditions still seem to not be well understood. (Also, I'm 1,000 percent sure those commercials are written, directed, and paid for by men.) At least, they aren't well understood by me and most of the women I know. This isn't because we're morons or because we're not trying to learn or because we're in denial. ("Meno-what? Why, I'm far too young for THAT!") Rather, it's because perimenopause and menopause are such long, confusing, drawn-out processes that we're not quite sure if it's happening or not. "It's kind of like having sex with a guy who has a small penis," my oversharing friend Jennifer said once. "You think you feel something inside you, but it's not big enough to really rock your world so you just go about your day." That colorful analogy sort of makes sense to me, and also, *name some names, Jennifer.*

One of the main issues of peri and menopause is that there isn't a set age when you can expect them. It's different for everyone because all bodies are different. Kind of like how we all got our first periods at various ages. I know I was thirteen when I got mine because I wrote "1980: The Year I Became a Woman" on a library book, then desperately tried to erase it because I'm terrified of librarians. But unlike the beginning of menstruation milestone, the inglorious end isn't something you can make plans around. It's as vague and capricious as Gen Z meme culture. You can't write a date on your calendar or track it with an app that tells you your exact egg stores at any given time. "Florida in October? No, thanks. I'll be down to my last three eggs by then, sliding hard into menopause and whew, I *really* don't want to hot flash in Orlando. What about Greenland? I hear Greenland's nice in the winter." Instead, you just have to wait for your body to do what your body's going to do.

The medical websites I've read say that menopause may begin "after forty" or "anywhere from thirty-five to sixty" or "usually around age fifty." Those numbers sound like speed limits, not actual scientific information. I know it's different for everyone, but you'd think the medical profession could narrow it down a little better. You'd think they could give us a bit of insight into what's actually happening. But maybe—*radical thought*—they can't because they don't *have* any insight. I fully suspect that the nebulous "Perimenopause" was created just to cover their asses. Just so they have something to diagnose when sweaty middle-aged women plop down on the exam table and complain about their various nagging symptoms.

"My waist is widening."

"Could be perimenopause."

"I can't sleep."

"Could be perimenopause."

"I have a recurring dream about making out with Jennifer Lawrence in a Target dressing room. She was all over me with her tongue."

"Please describe this dream to me in exact detail while I roll around on my little doctor stoolie with wheels, and yes, could be perimenopause."

Anything from moodiness to insomnia to slow metabolism can be chalked up/dismissed by doctors as "perimenopause." And women say "okay, thanks" when they shrug and tell us there's nothing we can do about it and oh, yeah, this discomfort might last ten years. What a load of sexist bullshit that is. We all know that if men went through any of this, even a second of it, there'd be a team of researchers with billion-dollar grants working like mad to determine how to cure perimenopause or at least alleviate the symptoms. Not only that, they'd also nail menopause's start down to the closest second for each individual dude. "Hey, Herb? Yeah, it's the boys down at the lab. Be sure to hit the bar on November 30th at 7:02 p.m. because that's when your reproductive system will officially close up shop, and you know what that means. FREE MENOPAUSE MOJITOS, MAN!"

Per Dr. Internet again, the official start to menopause, the whistle blow that calls the whole reproductive game, is when you don't get a period for twelve months. That *sounds* like an easy tracker. However, some women I know will go a few months without a period, then it suddenly breezes back in the door like it just returned from a carefree semester abroad. "'Ello! *C'est moi*! Deed you meese me?" Or their period will go into overdrive and last for weeks at a time. I've actually heard my friends use the word "gusher" to describe their late-forties periods. Like Jed Clampett's in their underpants, and he just struck oil. Yikes. But heavy, unpredictable cycles? Not getting a period and then suddenly getting one that won't stop? And no longer being able to rely on the cycle you've had for decades? Who the hell wants to deal with that? I know I don't. I had enough of that shit in junior high when I had to tie a shirt around my waist after getting an unexpected period in gym class. (Of course, it was on climb-the-rope day. It's always on climb-the-rope day.)

However, unlike my friends who are still buying maxi-pads, I haven't had a period for the past four years. Longer, by the time you read this. I mean, not to brag or anything. But the reason I don't get a period isn't because I prayed my time of the month away. "Dear God, if you take away my cramps, I promise to be somewhat nicer to my weird neighbor." Or because I went into menopause early. No, the reason I no longer get my monthly bill is thanks to the Awesome Magical Uterine Surgery I had to rid myself of the crazy period pain and dark moods that were becoming increasingly worse as I got older. Awesome Magical Uterine Surgery is also known as "endometrial ablation," and I believe it involves removing some of your uterine lining, so you still ovulate but you don't bleed every month. I wasn't really listening to my doctor when he explained it because my brain automatically shuts down when I hear more than three medical terms in a row. That's why I never know what's happening on *Grey's Anatomy*. But he reassured me it is safe, common, and easy, so I said sign me up.

The day of my procedure, I laid on a table at the medical office and they gave me an IV full of sweet, sweet drugs. Then I woke up a half hour later feeling well-rested and pleasantly stoned. So stoned that I didn't even mind when the doctor's office charged thirty-five-hundred dollars to my credit card because my insurance company considers the surgery that dramatically improved my quality of life "non-medically necessary." (Again, if men needed this surgery . . . well, you know.) I felt a little crampy for about a day, but that was it. Awesome Magical Uterine Surgery was a success, and I haven't had a period or a cramp since. No more "mommy has to lie in bed today because she has a tummy ache." The Angry Period Letter Lady is no more. I still get a little blue once a month, but it's manageable. Not like before when I stomped around my house, pissed off for no real reason, and bursting into tears at particularly poignant Whataburger commercials. "BUT HE'S JUST *SO HAPPY* WITH THAT DOUBLE PATTY MELT!" I recommend it to any woman who's a good candidate.

But while I love that I no longer get a period, that means that now I'll have to rely on various symptoms to know when I'm in perimenopause or menopause. Statistically and age-wise, I must be, but who really knows? There are a lot of symptoms. *A lot.* One article I read lists thirty-eight. That's an insane amount. No condition should have thirty-eight possible symptoms unless it's the bubonic plague or something you catch from aliens. Because thirty-eight possible symptoms means that, of course, you're going to have at least a couple. Anyone who's ever browsed WebMD and come away thinking they have an incurable disease that was eradicated in the 1800s knows that. But here are just some of the symptoms you may experience "in the months and years leading up to menopause":

- Irregular periods
- Vaginal dryness
- Irritability
- Tiredness
- Hot flashes
- Chills
- Night sweats
- Sleep problems
- Mood changes
- Weight gain and slowed metabolism

Oof. Let's break it down. But first, remove irregular periods and vaginal dryness from the list. Those symptoms are pertinent because they're exclusively related to lady parts. Nobody goes to any doctor besides their gynecologist to complain about their parched vagina. At least, I hope nobody does. Please don't bring up your dehydrated vajayjay with your dentist unless you want to hear that it's because you don't floss well enough. (Also, dry vagina reminds me of the time I bought ten tubes of K-Y Jelly and four pumpkins at the grocery store because I was writing a how-to article about jack-o-lantern carving, and I'd read that lube helps keep them fresh. Then, of course, I ran into three people from my neighborhood who saw that freakshow in my cart, and now they all avoid me because they think I'm into Halloween gourd orgies. Which is actually fine by me.)

Besides the vaginal things, the other symptoms on the list are valid, but they also seem to be less menopause and more Everyday Woman Issues. At least they are for me. Sleep problems? Tiredness? Irritability? I've experienced all of those to some extent my entire life, and I honestly don't know a single woman who hasn't. Of course, bad sleep and irritability ramp up when you're older, for sure. That's a common complaint. But that may also be because you're busy with your family and work and dealing with tons of adult stresses. You can't sleep because you're anxious, which leads to tiredness, which leads to irritability and tension, which leads to not sleeping well, and so on and so on. It's a vicious cycle that may or may not be related to perimenopause and menopause. Like I said, Everyday Woman Issues.

Most women, myself included, definitely experience more interrupted sleep in middle age. The infamous 4 a.m. wake-up witching hour. I haven't found any medical reason for this, but I'd guess it's hormone- and anxiety-related. However, one Google search I did (I can't stop! I'm addicted to Google!) told me that early morning wake ups "indicate that someone wants to communicate with you to make you understand the purpose of your life on earth," but judging by my inbox at that hour, that's only true if the "someone" is Frank from the mortgage company, who wants to tell me that the purpose of my life is paying off my home loan. But because so many of my friends are awake in the wee hours of the morning, all of us staring at the ceiling and questioning our life choices, we've even talked about starting a group text called "U Up, Bitch?" It's an epidemic. My friend Amanda, the one who eats on the treadmill at Orange Theory, has been waking up at 4 a.m. for years now. One day she looked even more tired than usual, which is saying something since she has four kids, elderly parents, a dog, and a full-time job.

"Are you not feeling well?" I asked with concern after I watched her dump two packets of sugar into her latte and stir it with her index finger.

"Yeah, I'm just exhausted because in the middle of the night my brain decided to revisit all of the financial decisions I've made since 1990," she yawned, "and then I spent a few moments in quiet panic that I'm going to die penniless and living at the YMCA, so I picked up my phone and researched cheap houses in Eastern Europe. Remind me to check my credit card statement because I might have put a deposit down on a fixer-upper in Moldova."

I don't even have to Google to know that European real estate websites see a spike in traffic at 4 a.m. when gobs of middle-aged American women are wide awake in bed weighing their options.

As far as the other symptoms on the list, a few friends have had night sweats and a couple more have experienced hot flashes, both of which they say is pure hell. It feels like "you're on fire from the inside." I'm not looking forward to any of that because I absolutely hate feeling too hot. Ask anyone who has ever encountered me in the summer months of Austin. I'm not exactly a delight when it gets above eighty degrees. So far, I've had some "hot flushes" which last just a couple minutes. They feel like I just stuck my head inside a sauna, then pulled it back out. They're not comfortable, but they're not awful, and I hope that's all I get.

The two symptoms that I definitely have and can't shake no matter what I try are weight gain and slowed metabolism. Nature's way of saying, "What's the point of having a sexy, visible waist if you can no longer make babies, Uggo?" Everything in the middle section of my body has spread and widened. This perceived loss of attractiveness and firmness and the frustration of gaining weight is a bitter pill to swallow for me and most women. Maybe that's why the peri/menopause phase of life often feels like it's more sad than empowering. It's yet another way middle-aged women are rendered obsolete and made to look like silly, old crones. One of the younger Real Housewives even used menopause as an insult when talking about her older castmates, saying something like, "This girl's trip is just me and a bunch of women who no longer get their periods." Ouch. Also, so what, Dorit? They're all still smarter than you, you ovulating dimwit who rents her outfits.

One day when I was twelve or thirteen, I was out shopping with my mom, and she saw a woman she knew. Sherry was standing in a corner of the store, her face covered in rivers of sweat, and she was rapidly fanning herself with a magazine. "She's going through The Change," my mom whispered to me with a look of sympathy and quickly pulled me in the other direction. "The Change of Life." I had no idea what that meant, and I didn't ask, but I could tell that whatever was happening to Sherry was bad. Was "The Change" like what happened to Michael J. Fox in *Teen Wolf*? I wondered later in my bedroom. Was my mom's friend Sherry about to grow fur all over her body and howl at the moon? Gross. No wonder we didn't want to be around her. But now that I'm Sherry's age, maybe even older, I think how different it would have been had my mom instead said, "Oh, look! Sherry's having a hot flash! How exciting that her body is entering a new phase of life! Here, go over there with this *Cosmopolitan* magazine and fan it to help cool her down. BUT DON'T READ THE SEX QUIZ." I don't blame my mom because obviously people weren't as open about things back then, but now we are or at least we should be. So maybe it's time we started celebrating menopause.

It's not *that* far-fetched of an idea. I mean, we celebrate a girl's first period now. Or some people do. There are period-themed party decorations, and Pinterest has pages full of tampon-themed food. (Which, no thanks. I do not want my cake with strings attached. Ba-dum-chh.) You can find countless books and websites and apps to support and inform girls, all offering reassurance that it's normal and natural for the female body to have a period. Can you imagine such a thing in the '80s? How that would have shaped us differently? Instead of scuttling to the bathroom with a tampon hidden in my pocket, I could have just yelled, "Gotta swap out my Kotex, classmates! It's a heavy flow day, so no rope climbing for me!" Now we're grown-ass women and we know better, so how about acknowledging, sharing, and cheering what's happening to us? How about we throw parties for The Change? Parties to say good-bye to the periods we've lived with for thirty-five plus years. They could be like retirement bashes with gold plaques that say, "Congratulations on a Reproductive Life Well Lived." Or "Bon Voyage, Aunt Flo!" Or "Your Time of the Month Has Come to An End, Friend." Or "You're Fresh Out of Eggs, Fucker!" The goodie bags could include mini-fans and a *Golden Girls* jigsaw puzzle and maybe a bottle of rum or two. Wouldn't that be fun? And empowering? How much happier would it feel to enter the post-menopausal years with our menopot bellies full of cake and laughter instead of shame and confusion? Hit me up, Hallmark. I got ideas.

As of this writing, I'm not yet in menopause, so you can hold off on my party planning. The only reason I know I'm not is because at my most recent annual exam/pap smear at age fifty-three, my doctor popped his head up from between the stirrups and cheerfully announced, "Well, you're not in menopause yet!" I didn't know what to say besides, "Oh, okay, thanks! USA! USA!" Then I stared at the limp gynecologist office mobile hanging above my head and wondered how he could tell that from just looking between my legs. Was there a countdown clock near my ovaries that I'd never seen before? A "Still going strong!" sign? Was Peri O'Menopause dancing a jig on my fallopian tubes? But then he solved the awkward mystery and chirped, "Mucus! You still have a good amount of mucus!" And then I felt uncomfortable and sweaty and couldn't make eye contact with him when he later handed me a brochure about colonoscopies and mentioned my infamous Always maxi-pad letter again. "It's still so funny!"

Right now, I'm holding steady and healthy, but like most women my age, I still get the occasional and/or regular symptom. Mostly backaches and sleepless nights and fussiness. I recently hurt my neck reaching for the remote. But maybe next year, the mucus (I don't even like *typing* that word) won't be as plentiful at my exam and maybe The Change will at long last happen for me. And when it does, you can bet your ass that I'm going to throw myself a big party. Eggs optional.

The Perfect Cocktails for Your Perimenopause Party

Not So Bloody Mary

But also, surprisingly bloody when you least expect it.

Gin and Tunics

Leave ~~nothing~~ everything to the imagination.

Martini Very, Very Dry

Garnish with an olive and a dab of K-Y Jelly.

Sex on the Beach with a Floppy Hat and SPF 85

Protect yourself before you wreck yourself.

Chin Hair of the Dog

10x magnifying mirror sold separately.

Ma'amosa

Bring your readers because this is no brunch for misses.

Eileen Fisher's Island Lemonade

Mix your lemons with your linen.

Dark and Stormy and Totally Over Your Shit

Been there, drank that.

Who You Calling "Old-Fashioned"?

You there in the Wham! concert t-shirt, that's who.

French 45ish

That's "Mademoiselle" to you.

The NeGROANi

Everything hurts, drink up.

Sloe Gin Frizz
Perfect for higher humidity and lowered shits to give.

Southern Comfort Before Fashion
Easy and breezy. You know, something that doesn't cinch at the waist.

Whiskey Dour
Life sucks and then you're fifty.

Hot Flash Toddy
Hot Girl Summer, only make it year-round.

The Whiskery Nipple
One part whiskey, one part tweezers. Cheers!

CHAPTER THIRTEEN

I'M WEARING DECADES NOW

One hot summer day, I called my friend Kathy to see if she wanted to hang out at the mall for a couple of hours because I had some free time. She immediately answered "Yes!" because she was bored at home, but also because she needed to find a prom dress. "You can help me pick one out," she said. "It's always more fun to have someone with you. You know, so you don't end up crying in the dressing room and buying something hideous that makes you look like a lump." We decided we'd meet at the JCPenney at the "good" mall in town. The great mall in town has a Neiman-Marcus; the bad mall, a Long John Silver's. We knew the level of mall that worked for us.

About an hour later, we found each other at the entrance to "Jacques Pennet." We wandered upstairs to the Junior's section bursting with jeans, t-shirts, dresses, and the cheap costume jewelry that turns your skin green and appears on government health department recall lists. We browsed our way through, touching various articles of highly flammable clothing, assessing, shrugging, then moving on. We finally found two racks in the back that were jammed with shiny, solid-colored satin prom dresses. Most of the dresses were covered in cheap lace or glittery accessories or both. It was like a nest of molting tropical birds. They weren't awful dresses, but they weren't great dresses, either. All of them were too pink, too short, too flimsy for Kathy's taste. For mine too, and I wasn't even in the market for a prom dress. Nobody had invited me to a prom. We weren't totally surprised to strike out at JCPenney, though, because they're not widely known for their *haute couture.*

We left the store empty handed, then aimlessly wandered the mall a bit, passing the pretzel stands and the lemonade stands, tons of moms with strollers trying to get in a workout, and the roving bands of teenagers that make adults nervous. We finally ended up in the perfume-clouded cosmetics department at Macy's because I wanted to look at the makeup. I was desperate to find something to cover my pimples. My face was broken out everywhere, even on my jawline, which is a cruel place for acne. A friend of mine calls it "Neckne," a word I'd enjoy if I didn't have to experience it. I picked up a bottle of light beige foundation that looked like it might work, and said, "Excuse me? How much for this one?" to the woman behind the counter. At least I thought it was a woman. She could have been a bear or an alien. It was hard to tell because her face was shellacked within an inch of her life with the products she sold.

"Good choice! That one is wonderful! It's sixty dollars a bottle."

"Huh. I'll think about it," I said, quickly putting the bottle back down, embarrassed by my sticker shock. "Sixty dollars? Who'd pay sixty dollars for four ounces of glorified poster board paint?" I whispered to Kathy. "Let's get out of here."

We bummed around a few other stores for a bit, not finding anything too exciting, then we each bought a soda and sat down in the food court to gossip. That was the real reason we were at the mall. We talked about our diets, the latest movies we'd seen and wanted to see, and how we definitely weren't interested in the one about sexy vampires because it just looked stupid. Jeff Goldblum as a fly? Sexy. Anyone as a vampire? Not sexy. We talked about her boyfriend and what he said to her on the phone the night before, and we both agreed that he's a really good guy. So sweet! And, of course, like every mall conversation ever between two girlfriends, we spent a few minutes discussing the hotness of Rob Lowe. Discussing Rob Lowe at the mall is required by law.

Tired of walking around and talked out, we said good-bye to each other by the Sears (there's no fancy way to say Sears, I've tried) and promised to call each other later. Between the shopping and the company and the catching up, it was the perfect 1986 afternoon.

Only it happened in 2018.

My fun girlfriend mall hang was one of those special days you sometimes get in life. A rarified moment when you find yourself doing something that feels true to who you are on the inside, not who you look like on the outside—when the years vanish and the younger part of you comes back to the surface, if just for a few hours. There's probably a German word for this phenomenon, but I don't know what it is because I took French in high school, then Spanish in college, and boy, did that screw me up *tres malo*. But what I'm trying to say is that on that day at the mall, I felt like my sixteen-year-old self, even though I was in my fifty-year-old body. And if (and hopefully when) that happens to you, it's a pretty damn great thing.

When I actually was my sixteen-year-old self, I spent most Saturdays at the Meadowood Mall in Reno, Nevada, with my best friend, Megan. Money from our after-school jobs burning a hole in our pockets, we'd drive to the mall, blasting music from the tape deck of my powder blue Chevy Nova. I'd find the right kind of parking space—one that I didn't need to back out of because my Chevy Nova didn't reverse (long story—thanks, Mom and Dad!)—then we'd go inside and head right to our favorite store, The Limited. We shopped there so often that we knew their inventory better than their employees.

"Uh, excuse me, Patty, but why did you move the rack of fluorescent orange sweatshirts two feet to the left? There's far less foot traffic over there."

Every week we'd grab armfuls of the latest 1985 fashion, like Shaker sweaters, giant striped blouses, and leggings. Leggings *with stirrups.* Yeehaw. It was all atrocious and cheap and unflattering, but like every teenager ever to teenage, we thought we looked good. We thought we looked like we'd just stepped out of a John Hughes movie. (But not *Pretty in Pink* because we didn't fully appreciate Duckie and Andie's thrift store chic yet.) Once done with our shopping and most of our paychecks, we'd spend whatever money was left on lunch at the Marie Callender's restaurant down the street. We always chose Marie's because at sixteen we didn't yet know that sugar, white flour, and entire chocolate pies weren't good things to put in your body. Why would we? We never gained weight. Not really. Man, I miss that metabolism. I miss *a* metabolism.

Megan and I would sit in our booth at Marie's, with our frosted pink lipstick and our big, poufy perms, hair lightened by Sun-In, polishing off our thirty-five-thousand-calorie lunches, and wonder why the boys at school didn't appreciate our very obvious sex appeal. "To be fair, I don't appreciate their sex appeal, either," Megan said once. "But that's only because they don't have any." "Sex appeal" was how we said "hot." At the time, we didn't want to have sex with *anyone.* Well, besides George Michael, and that didn't work out for us despite years of fantasizing. RIP.

Other regular topics of conversation at Marie Callender's included the sex appeal of Rob Lowe (legally required), the makeup we used to cover our pimples, why that makeup never worked, more Rob Lowe, movies about sexy human flies, and our tragic lack of boyfriends and how we couldn't wait until college where we knew we'd be better understood by older men. "Guys in college are *so* much more mature," I remember pontificating, like an idiot who would find out how wrong she was her first weekend at the University of Oregon when a fraternity guy in a toga puked on her feet. (Reader: I dated him.) Megan and I would then speed home in my Chevy Nova, bellies full, wallets empty, big hair blowing, blasting a Go-Go's or INXS cassette. We especially loved singing along to The Go-Go's song "Vacation" because all we ever wanted was to shop, hang out, gossip, and eat pies in our stirrup leggings. It was a nice teenage life.

So. Now you know why my day with Kathy took me back. There were a few notable differences in 2018, however. First, I wasn't sixteen years old in 2018, but thirty-four years older. A big old funky fifty. Second, it was unusual for me to be there. These days I only go to a mall if I need something like a new bra because mine are twenty years old and look like they have been chewed on by a family of mice. Which they maybe have been, considering the state of my closet. (I found a plant growing in the corner once. I'm not proud.) I only resort to shopping at the mall when I can't find what I want online. Most people do the same, which is why a lot of malls are now closing or being repurposed as community colleges. (Thoughts and prayers to anyone who goes to school in an old Spencer's Gifts.) And as for having any money in my pocket to burn? Ha. No. Any money I have to spare now has either been put into the kids' college funds or into our retirement savings or used to pay for some luxury like new kitchen grout or propane. How depressing is that? My pie money now pays for heat. The joy of working all week, then spending all of my hard-earned money on the weekend is long, long gone.

Though I was looking at makeup to cover my pimples, just like I did when I was a teenager, the reason the foundation I picked up in Macy's was sixty dollars is because I now need one that covers my wrinkles too. How awesome is that? Wrinkles and pimples are the yin and yang of a fifty-year-old woman's face. The regular drugstore Cover Girl shit won't cut it anymore. I now need the tough stuff. Industrial stuff. And any product that manages to smooth out a middle-aged face requires more pigment, more chemicals, and probably a few rounds of nuclear testing in an underground lab to make it effective. Hence, the high-ticket price. I know Bobbi Brown isn't hurting for cash.

But the biggest difference in my 2018 trip to the mall and my trips to the mall in the '80s is that when I was sixteen, I listened to The Go-Go's in my Chevy Nova on the way there, but as a fifty-year-old, I was actually meeting up with my friend Kathy Valentine, *who is the bassist for the Rock and Roll Hall of Fame–inducted Go-Go's.* Oh, and what's more, *she wrote the song "Vacation."* That's right, I'm now good friends with the rock star I listened to in my beater car when I was in high school. Yes, this is a brag and not a humble one, either. What a world.

Oh, and the reason Kathy and I were looking for a prom dress wasn't because she somehow got invited to a prom as a prank or because she was going to some retro Mom Prom fiftieth birthday party. (Which I'm dying to be invited to, FYI. Anyone throwing one of these, please ask me, and I'll be there with bells and a wrist corsage on.) It was because she wanted something fun to wear for The Go-Go's sold-out shows at the Hollywood Bowl, and she thought a trendy party dress would be fun on stage. Yep. The freaking Hollywood Bowl. I've been to the Hollywood Bowl, but nowhere even near the stage, much less on it. I can honestly say that searching for a prom dress with a Go-Go was the most exciting thing I've ever done in a department store. Hands down. And I once sold a satin comforter to a member of Whitesnake when I worked in the Macy's bedding department.

As for why we were talking about Rob Lowe when he is clearly no longer a teenage heartthrob and we're no longer teenagers with throbbing hearts? He's still hot and has a lot of *sex appeal*, but most fifty-year-old women don't spend a lot of time discussing male movie stars. At least I hope they don't. No, the reason we were talking about Rob is because Kathy mentioned that she'd seen him at his Austin show where he spoke about the books he's written. He's an author now because even he couldn't continue a career of playing the no-good heartbreaker who cheats on his girlfriend with her mom. I said to her, "I know you went because I saw the picture you posted on Instagram of you and Rob backstage. How'd that happen?" In my cluelessness, I figured that maybe she'd won a contest or something. That's the only way I'd meet Rob Lowe, anyway. Like some charity prize or Queen for a Day contest winner. But no. "Well, Rob and I are friends. We went so my teenage daughter could meet him." She. And. Rob. Are. Friends. What the hell. I mean, no offense to Megan, who I love and still keep in touch with, but that pretty much blows everything we ever discussed at Marie Callender's out of the water. Even Megan's dramatic retelling of her kiss during theater class rehearsals of *Ordinary People* with a boy named Mike, who is now happily married to a man named Ted, doesn't come close. Sorry, Megan, I'll send you a pie.

It wasn't until that parallel nostalgia-bomb of a day at the mall that I *truly* understood why older people say they still feel like teenagers inside. I've always felt the age I am. I mean, at least I mostly have. I don't know what a twenty-five-year-old or a thirty-five-year-old "should" feel like, but I know that I don't act a lot younger than my chronological age. I've grown, I've matured, and I've experienced a lot of the world in my fifty-plus years, so it'd be weird if I still behaved like I did in 1985 when I hung out near the Orange Julius hoping that the dorky boy working there would finally notice me. (He did, but only after I started choking on a smoothie.) What I feel on the inside—adult burdens and responsibilities and concerns—shows up on my outside via dark circles, frown lines, and gray hair. The worries I have now are far weightier than hoping the deconstructed sweater I bought at The Limited is the same one the popular girls at school own. I'm no longer the teenage girl desperate to know if her life will be as exciting as she thinks she deserves it to be. I still have hope for life to surprise me, but it's different.

But on that day at the mall, walking around with my cool friend, laughing at shared jokes, searching through racks of party dresses, gossiping about movie stars and boyfriends and movie-star friends, I actually kind of did feel like that sixteen-year-old girl. Like a vast, exciting future was ahead of me.

Until it was time to go pick up my husband from his colonoscopy. Because that's the reason I had two hours to kill that day, at the good mall in town.

CHAPTER FOURTEEN

I'M WEARING A SLOWER PACE NOW

My parents have a certain damning phrase they sometimes say when they're talking about one of their friends or relatives. It's not a mean or insulting remark, although they deploy those with increasing frequency. My mom has become quite fond of loudly declaring, "Those pants sure aren't doing her any favors" whenever she thinks the occasion calls for her fashion judgment. She and Chris had a lot of fun playing Freelance Fashion Police on a family cruise we once took. No, the particular phrase I'm talking about is more of a status report. One that informs me to not count on whoever it is for any long-term plans.

"Remember your high school teacher, Hank Thomas?" my mom will begin. "We saw him at the store the other day." Then, before I can ask how he's doing and if he's still in the barbershop quartet that everybody in town hates, she'll lower her voice, widen her eyes, and lean in to say, "*He's really slowed down.*" I'm never quite sure if that means he has mere hours to live or it's just a heads-up to not ask Hank to be the anchor on my four-by-four relay team, but I do know that for my mom and dad "slowing down" isn't a good thing. Not a good thing at all. The only time it's been a plus in their estimation was when I stopped trying to microwave cakes. "It won't kill you to actually use your oven for once, you know."

This phrase of theirs has been on my mind a lot recently because, well, I've really slowed down. At least I think I have; I have no real proof. I never timed how long it took me to make a bed when I was twenty-five, so I don't know if it takes me longer now that I'm fifty. Plus, there's the fact that I never make my own bed, so that's probably a bad example to give in the first place. The only time I actually made beds was when I worked in the bedding department at a San Fernando Valley Macy's in my twenties. Part of my job was to create "inviting bedscapes" on the floor model beds, and I was terrible at that pillow sham bullshit. That's also the job where I met Ray Parker Jr. of *Ghostbusters* fame when I sold him a red comforter, handed him his receipt, and whispered, "I ain't 'fraid of no sheets," and then my boss Janice pulled me into the stockroom and threatened to fire me for "acting inappropriately with a celebrity customer" even though she apparently didn't have a problem when my co-worker June asked Marlena from *Days of Our Lives* to autograph a shower curtain. But I digress. My point is that lately I've been feeling like I'm not as quick and nimble as I used to be, and I don't know if that's normal.

My same-age friends who complain about everything under the sun haven't fessed up to feeling slow. Not even when I said, "I'm morphing into a turtle. Look at how long it takes me to lift my wine glass" at our most recent happy hour. They probably ignored me because it didn't seem like I was really struggling to polish off half a bottle of chardonnay, but still—what gives? They bitch about gray eyebrow hairs and hot flashes and all of the other aging indignities, so why aren't they talking about this? Or am I the only one feeling both mentally and physically stuck in molasses?

I decided to ask my OB/GYN about my sluggishness at my last annual exam. I've been his patient for over twenty years, and I hardly ever bug him about anything, so I figured I was due to bend his ear a little. Sometimes when I'm sitting on the exam table wearing nothing but a paper sheet and a grimace, paging through a *Good Housekeeping* from 1979, I hear him in the next room with another patient and it sounds like a cocktail party. "Ah ha ha! You are just delightful! Care for another gin martini while I get the speculum out of the deep freeze, my dear? A bite of *crudité*?" Because I'm such an easy patient, I assumed that I was his favorite and therefore assumed he'd move heaven and earth to find the answer for me. I expected he'd gasp, clutch his figurative pearls, then immediately pull out reference books, email his doctor pals, and maybe dial up the Mayo Clinic VIP hotline. But no, Dr. Private Parts just glanced up from his rolling doctor stool and said, "Blood test. That'll tell us if something's out of whack."

"Oh, is 'out of whack' a medical term now?" I asked, feeling a bit spurned. "I guess I haven't heard that one on *General Hospital* yet. Thanks, Doc." Ten minutes later, I was squeezing a stress ball in the lab while a tech named Zelda plunged a needle into my arm and chirped, "You have really shy veins! They're hiding from me! Come out, come out, veins!" At least she gave me a cookie at the end of it.

A week later, my blood test results arrived via email, and I eagerly opened the file to read them over. At last, I'd know that something was clinically wrong with me! I'd finally have proof that the reason it took me twenty minutes to fill out a three-question survey about my most recent Pizza Hut experience was medical! I crossed my fingers that the results would show I had some rare disease that yes, was tragic but also curable. Like a condition on *House*, or one those sad-yet-beautiful girls in YA books get. Maybe it'd be so bad that I'd be required to take long, poignant walks through a fragrant garden while listening to a song John Legend wrote for me. Alas, no such luck. My stupid blood test showed that I'm in perfect health. Triglycerides and diglycerides and all of the other glycerides are in the normal range. Even my thyroid, something both of my sisters and my mother have issues with, was happily lounging in the "hey, don't blame me, asshole, I'm fine" area. Of course I realize how spectacularly lucky that is. *Spectacularly lucky*. But also, *shit*, because what was making me feel slow?

"You don't eat enough fruit," my husband said. "The last time I saw you eat a banana was 1991, and I think it was covered in chocolate."

"That's not true."

"Oh, yeah, you're right. I apologize. It was an apple covered in chocolate. If I remember correctly, you chased it with a Diet Coke."

Despite my alleged fruit deficit, I know it's not my diet that's the problem. My food intake is pretty balanced. I mean, I'm not a vegan or a Keto fanatic, but I take two gummy vitamins every day that are Formulated for Women. A lack of iron can cause fatigue, but my blood test showed that my iron level was fine. Plus, I eat a lot of iron-rich food, like spinach. Okay, that's a lie, but dark chocolate is also considered iron-rich by some websites. None of that mattered anyway because my problem isn't that I'm particularly tired. It's just that I'm not as quick as I used to be. Especially mentally.

I had an impressive immediate recall for most of my life, but once I got into my late forties, it was like a fuzzy cloud drifted in and took hold between the questions and my answers. I'm not talking about my memory, although that's also an issue I wrote about elsewhere in here. At least I think I did; let me know if you see it. No, what's happening to me is more of a speed thing. There's now a one- or two-second pause that didn't used to be there. It's like my brain has an involuntary delay like TV networks use in case someone yells "Motherfucker!" during a quinoa cooking demonstration with Al Roker. I know one or two seconds doesn't seem like a lot of time, but it concerns me because those seconds never used to be there.

Recently I was on the phone with my credit card company dealing with some issue, probably a three-hundred-dollar spa charge I forgot about, and Sue B. asked for my social security number. I know my social security number really well and have for at least thirty years. But before answering, I had a moment of hesitation while the squirrels in my head ran around trying to conjure it up. "I got a five! Jimmy, do you have a two?" What the hell? Another recent night, I was watching *Jeopardy!* with my teenage son Jack, and knew I knew all of the answers in the Pacific Coast States category, but they didn't make the move from my brain to my mouth fast enough to say them before he did. It upset me because I've always prided myself on being quick on the draw, especially when competing with children. Fortunately, I beat him in the Bible category, but only because my strategy is to yell, "WHAT IS DEUTERONOMY!" at every answer until I'm right.

I finally got some confirmation that I'm not alone in this slowness when my friend Jane, an Austin writer and mother of three, admitted to me that she's experienced a mental slowing down too. That made me feel a lot better. However, unlike me, Jane loves it that her brain isn't as quick as it used to be. "It takes me longer to respond to people now," she said, "But that means I can be more mature and thoughtful with my words." I can get behind that. Both she and I have been around long enough to know that the first thing that pops into our heads isn't necessarily the best thing to utter. (See: 2009 when Wendi meets a journalist in person and says, "Oh my god, that's really your hair and not a wig! Wow!") Jane says she's no longer in such a rush to impress, or charm, or be the first to answer now. She's more relaxed in her interactions than when she was younger. I thought about this, and realized that I kind of am too. The nervousness I used to feel when talking to people is mostly gone because I'm in my fifties and don't give as much of a shit, so I no longer just stammer anything to fill the air. That kind of slowness is a good thing.

Lest you be too impressed by Jane because I made it sound like she's a wise and rational role model, she's not. She's kind of a dick. Her most favorite thing in the entire world to do is antagonize a Gen Zer or millennial in a hurry. One time we were walking on Austin's Congress Avenue after lunch, and I watched in delighted shock as she intentionally stepped directly into the path of a self-important thirty-year-old professional woman who was clomping down the middle of the sidewalk, head in her phone. This caused said professional to lock it up and almost fall down and rip out the knees of her Instagram jeans. I thought it was maybe an accident until Jane exclaimed, "Oops, sorry! Better pay attention!" with an evil glint in her eye. Another time I watched her kick a scooter some young tank top was parking, just for the hell of it. But her favorite activity happens whenever she's in a busy coffee place. After the crazed barista asks for her order, Jane will silently count to sixty before answering. "I can feel the nervous energy in the room amp up the longer it takes me," she says. "It's fantastic. One of these days someone's going to bust a piercing or hit me with their phone." On the one hand, it's great that Jane has found a way to entertain herself in her dotage. On the other hand, she'll probably be (mostly deservedly) shivved with a coffee stirrer before she turns fifty-five.

I was happy Jane anecdotally validated that my slower response time is age-appropriate, but I also got confirmation via a story I heard on NPR. (Nothing says "bursting with youthful vitality" like "a story I heard on NPR.") Some researcher/author was on talking about his new book where he claims that brains no longer form new ideas once they turn fifty. He said that instead of coming up with any original solutions or creations, we oldies instead call upon the wisdom and experience we've gleaned over the years to solve problems. At first, I believed him because I tend to believe everything I hear on NPR. If a calming, melodious voice said Elvis is still alive and working as a shuttle bus driver in Ohio, I'd smile and whisper, "I knew it, King!" But it's certainly not a stretch to think that my brainwaves aren't as loaded with innovation as they used to be, and it's not because they've atrophied from watching at least two-hundred hours of *The Real Housewives of New York City*. They're just old brainwaves. But then my graying gray matter thought about what he said a bit more and what his book is about and his proposed theory, and I decided he's full of shit.

Here's why: while I appreciate the idea that people over fifty have a wealth of experience and knowledge to call upon when faced with a new situation, it's not like I now rely exclusively on 1980s knowledge to handle things. "The dishwasher is broken? Better get out the phone book and let my fingers do the walking to find an appliance repairman! Hey, Culligan Man!" I don't think I've seen a phone book since 2001. It's true that at my age I'm not innovative enough to invent something like an app, but I never *was* innovative enough for that kind of thing. At my peak intelligence, I couldn't even invent an appetizer. But of course, I know how to use an app to get shit fixed. I know how to learn new ways to solve problems—especially if the consequence of not doing so is washing dishes by hand. The author on NPR no doubt had his theories backed up by scientific evidence, but I wonder how much anecdotal evidence he included?

Maybe those of us over fifty aren't exactly *bursting* with original ideas, but we're still creating plenty of books and movies, and, in my case, Instastories about cats dancing to Duran Duran, and forming many other creative plans to deal with an ever-changing world. It takes nimble thinking when you're quite possibly trying to keep children and parents and a career and a few pets alive. Besides that, it's

I'M WEARING TUNICS NOW

not like anyone these days can really depend on previous experience to tell us how to handle current situations. Most of what's happening now is unprecedented. As I write this, the world is in the thick of the COVID-19 pandemic, and the President of the United States just suggested that drinking bleach will cure it. What. The. Fuck. My brain doesn't have the wisdom to deal with a steaming pile of idiocy like that. Nobody's does, no matter how old and experienced or young and supple their brains might be. It's looney tunes.

But while this mental slowing down of mine is a pain in the ass, it's nothing compared to the physical decline that kicked in during the Great Quarantine of 2020. If my parents saw me moving around, they'd no doubt lean in to whisper to each other.

"She used to vacuum a lot faster, don't you think? It just took her twenty minutes to do the living room."

"I know, Wayne, but let's just be happy she decided to vacuum for once."

This physical decline has probably been happening for years, but it took me a while to realize I was moving slower because nobody moves too quickly in Texas. It's devil's ass crack hot. One July night I saw a man buy an ice cream cone that melted in the time it took him to walk twenty feet to a bench. (Just one of the many reasons I eat my ice cream in a single gigantic bite, like a Labrador.) It took a visit to New York City for me to finally realize how plodding I'd become when I saw everyone zipping around like they were trying to lose a hitman who was tailing them. No matter where you are in NYC, people move fast. Even senior citizens cross against the light because it's bullshit to wait two seconds for the Walk signal. On past visits, I've been able to adapt to the local speed and keep up nicely, but not this time. We were there for a week, walking miles every day, and every night I had to pop Motrin because my knees and back were killing me. I also had swollen ankles, which my husband called "cankles" and then I didn't talk to him for a while and then he called them "crankles." But it was weird to be the kind of person who needs to sit on a bench in the park to rest up a little. I'd *never* done that before. But here's the thing: it wasn't awful. I actually liked taking that break because it made me realize that it's okay to not always rush. It's okay to just look around and relax and let your soft pretzel digest a bit—it's nice even.

I've thought about that visit a lot, and it's led me to a decision: I'm embracing my newfound slowness. What other options do I have? Push myself until I hurt? Try to win some race against younger people that doesn't get me anywhere? Cocaine? No, and not just because I gave away the Van Halen coke mirror I bought at the 1978 North Dakota state fair years ago. What I will do is work out as much as I can to stay fit and accept that sometimes parts of my body will hurt. I'll keep my brain active with brain games like Sudoku, which I'll then get frustrated by and stab with my pen because those numbers make *no damn sense*. Sudoku is *bullshit*. (#TeamWordle) I'll remind myself to appreciate that it takes me longer to respond, and that I shouldn't feel bad if I'm keeping someone waiting for an answer. Why not reframe this slowing down of mine and make it a good thing? Rather than a defeat, it's simply nature's way of making me stop and see the world in more detail and feel more grateful for what's in it: flowers, trees, birds, mimes, what have you. There's so much beauty to take in, and guess what? It's not exclusively on my phone.

In the many times I've visited New York City, there was one iconic citizen that I'd never seen until that day my feet hurt so much that I sat down on the park bench. The relative silence of the afternoon was broken when I heard a skittering noise in the leaves. I looked right, then left, to see what it was, and there, staring right at me with the bored expression all locals seem to wear when they see a tourist, was a giant gray rat. My first one. I gasped like I'd just met Queen Elizabeth II. If I'd been rushing around town like a thirty-year-old full of health, vigor, and muscle tone, like I had in years past, if I'd been too busy to stop and smell the roses—or at least the hot dogs—the two of us would have never met and locked eyes.

(Let the John Legend ballad begin.)

CHAPTER FIFTEEN

I'M WEARING A PARTY HAT NOW

We had a birthday party ritual when my boys were small. Each year, about a month before their big days, we'd sit down for a serious discussion about what that year's theme would be. Dinosaurs? Baseball? Animals? The possibilities were endless. I loved creating parties around their chosen theme, especially the year we hired an unlicensed Texas "amateur zoo" to show up at our neighborhood park, and one of the wallabies got loose for ten amazing minutes. ("Y'all need to help me catch that bouncy li'l fucker! Oops, sorry, kids.") So that's why, when I was approaching fifty a couple of years ago and talking about maybe throwing myself a party, my son Jack asked what the theme would be.

"Is the sweet release of death a theme?"

"Uh, I don't think so, but maybe?"

"Well, ask Dad if it is because the only other idea I have is wearing Mardi Gras beads while I get a colonoscopy."

You might think that the person who sobbed on her thirtieth birthday because she thought most of her life was behind her wouldn't handle turning fifty well, and you would be right. Okay, sort of right. I did indeed begin to dread that particular whopper of a decade birthday when I turned forty-nine. For an entire year, I fretted about being "so old" and "decaying" and "twice the age of Miley Cyrus as well as her dad's classic 1992 song "Achy Breaky Heart," which is a bizarre coincidence. But then something completely unexpected happened. As the calendar pages flew off the wall like they do in the movies and the scary date got closer, I started to feel—kind of happy? And excited? And I wasn't even medicated.

The reason I felt optimistic is simple: I knew I was lucky. By the age of fifty, I'd lived a lot of life. Like *a lot*. A hell of a lot. There wasn't even remote control for the TV when I was born, and now I can probably land the space shuttle with my iPhone 13. *Houston, we have a problem, and her name is Wendi and she's pushing buttons.* I'd survived five entire decades, and that's a milestone to be celebrated, not embarrassed about. After all, nobody makes it to that age unscathed. By fifty, your scorecard is filled with triumphant wins and devastating losses and maybe a few forfeits because you were on your period that day and refused to climb the rope. I had countless friends and family who'd suffered from illness, or they'd gone through horrible circumstances, or they'd lost their lives, so for me to whine and hide because I was a bit too old for my liking? For me to cry in my closet like a baby because I was turning fifty? Nope. No way. That's what an asshole would do, and, like I once yelled at the snotty woman who asked me why I was bothering to put my cart back into the cart corral at Target, I AM NOT AN ASSHOLE. I decided to embrace my big five-oh with my welcoming, if slightly untoned, arms.

Like all milestone birthdays, fifty sent me into a period of moody self-reflection, but this time my dark mood was brief because it'd been twenty years since I turned thirty—twenty mostly happy years which were a blur of kids and jobs and houses and friends and like one hundred *Fast & Furious* movies. Unlike thirty or even forty, the fifth decade hit different. This decade didn't carry a Sea Breeze sting that left me gasping for air until my emotions and face finally cooled down. And here's the reason why: I now fit into the world that I'd spent years working to build. I now fit into *myself*.

At fifty, I was no longer the insecure Hollywood assistant embarrassed to be from North Dakota, or the new mom hoping someone at Gymboree would talk to me, or the blogger writing sponsored posts for a free frozen yogurt coupon. I had a part-time social media job I liked, some freelance work, and I was finally contributing to our college and retirement savings, which meant fewer 3 a.m. money panics. Chris and I were happy and getting along, which varies by the day, of course, but we had way more good times than bad and that's something you can't always expect in a marriage that's approaching thirty years. My adorable little boys were no longer little, but they were both doing well and finding their paths in life, and now sleeping until noon and doing their own laundry, so I was back to being well-rested. Plus, I was writing good satire that was getting attention, we were traveling a lot, and it was an exciting time in our country because an eminently qualified woman was running for president, and there was no possible way she was going to lose to the Orange Moron. Why *not* celebrate? Why *not* break out the good china and sit on the fancy sofa and drink the expensive champagne I'd been saving for a special occasion? I was ready to party.

All of that said, I for sure didn't want to become a Birthday Queen. You know the type. They announce on the first of the month that their birthday is imminent, then remind you approximately 23,104 times after that about their special day. "Just forty-three days until I'm thirty-six!" "It's Leo Season!" "Guess whose birthday is coming soon?!" Yours, Janice. We all know it's yours because you've fucking told us every day since your last birthday that you're on another "trip around the sun" like you're some kind of space explorer in a linen blazer.

Yes, that sounds crabby, and that's because it is. It's hard to avoid the Birthday Queens due to Instagram and Facebook. It can feel like everyone else is always ringing in their big birthdays with a super fun party or trip with their best gal pals. I don't go a day online without seeing a group shot of sloppy drunk women with runny mascara celebrating something like #omgJill's40th! These pics seem fancy and exotic and sometimes a tad worrisome, especially when you glimpse Vlad the underage stripper holding Jill's Mastercard in the background, but they've now become *de rigueur* for a certain class of American. Don't just age, age with a hashtag! It definitely creates FOMO.

FOMO was probably the reason why I decided to celebrate my fortieth birthday with a "girls' trip." ("We're over the age of seventeen, so it *should* be called a Women's Trip," I was fond of grandly announcing before I was repeatedly told to shut up.) At forty, I was heavily into that mom life. I had a Volvo, a c-section scar, the theme from *Dora the Explorer* permanently stuck in my head, and if I carried business cards at the time, they would have said, "Wendi Aarons: Suburban Wanker," and I would have stuffed them in every "Win a Free Lunch!" jar in every Applebee's in town. All pretenses of being young and hip seemed long gone, so I eagerly planned a girls' weekend trip to calm, centering, and monochromatic brown Santa Fe to celebrate.

My accomplices on that trip to New Mexico were my youngest sister, Amy; my mom, Sharon; two friends from high school, Karen and Megan; and Renee, a mom friend from Austin who I met when our first sons were in a baby playgroup. An easygoing, fun bunch. We all arrived on different flights, then met up in our cute downtown hotel that was comprised of little adobe *casitas*, like you'd expect to find in Santa Fe. Every single building in that city is made out of clay—even the Starbucks. Mention aluminum siding to the mayor and she'd say, "What's that? Our airport is made out of pottery!" I love it there.

That "girls' weekend" was filled with hiking, shopping, eating Santa Fe's specialty—red and green Christmas enchiladas—until we were stuffed, and then my favorite activity: a visit to the beautiful Georgia O'Keeffe museum. I'm a huge fan of Georgia and her work, and not just because she was far more wrinkled than I'll ever be. At least, I hope that remains the case. Time will tell because, like her, I'm far too busy being an artistic genius to bother with SPF 50. But besides a brief misadventure in the forest while in search of a Native American village that my sister thought consisted of treehouses (it did not) and was built in the 1600s (it was not) and served wine and cheese (huh?), everything went well. On the night of my birthday, my mom, sister, and friends presented me with a vanilla cake, and we talked and laughed into the early morning in our comfy *casita*. It was the perfect trip with the perfect mix of people.

That's not always the case.

I've heard stories about rival alliances forming before the plane even takes off. It can be like *Survivor*, only with an all-middle-aged-women cast, sponsored by chardonnay on the rocks and erratic mood swings. (Yes, I know I just described the *Real Housewives* franchise.) Whitney and Anne don't drink, so they're avoiding party girls Brittney and Jane, who are avoiding smokers Lily and Tammy, who hate Mary because she's a Republican who not only voted for Ted Cruz but had a friggin' *yard sign*, so it's all a bit awkward when the birthday girl gets them all up on the karaoke stage to sing a Wilson Phillips song. "Hold on for one more day," indeed. More like hold on for one more hour before you "accidentally" spill your gin and tonic all over Jennifer's calfskin ankle boots that she won't stop bragging about.

When my friend Shauna went to Napa Valley for a friend's fortieth, the group was having a good time until they got a few glasses of pinot noir under their belts and two of the women discovered they'd been sleeping with the same man. Only one of them was married to him. Drinks were thrown, hair was pulled, tears were shed. Bravo Andy's dream come true. I'm surprised nobody sent him the cell phone video as an audition reel. Shauna said it was an awful scene, and the birthday girl couldn't stop crying. She also told me later that while the cheating revelation did indeed wreck the entire trip, and everyone went home early, she also got a great glute workout from pulling apart the women who were wrestling on the winery floor. We Gen Xers, always looking for that silver lining.

Back to my Big Five-Oh.

I started the celebration with a mini-girls' weekend in Lake Tahoe with my mom and two sisters, Lisa and Amy. We were lucky to get to stay in my friend Kelly's lakefront home, which is actually more of a compound with one main house, five historic cabins, and the constant danger of roaming bears to keep you on your toes. (Tip: By this age, if at all possible, you should know at least a few people who own lakefront homes.) The three days we spent up there were relaxed and silly and fun, and I wasn't even that upset when Amy presented me with a box of Depends and those giant plastic sunglasses elderly people put on over their regular glasses when they're driving. (They, um, actually work pretty well.) It was a wonderful weekend in Tahoe, and the best part was that this time I didn't do any hysterical sobbing on the way back down the mountain. My only issue was a slight headache from drinking cheap champagne mimosas for forty-eight straight hours while playing cards, but I'm used to that. I've been living that way *for years*. I spent the last morning of the weekend sitting on a mossy rock, staring at the gorgeous, deep blue lake, and listening to my mom yelling, "If you're fifty, that makes me ancient! Hoo boy!" It was perfect.

Back home, I excitedly started to plan my birthday party. It was the first party I'd ever thrown for myself. I think because it always seemed like a narcissistic thing to do (which it totally isn't), but mostly because I never liked being the center of attention. It was excruciating enough to have random servers in a mid-range seafood restaurant sing "Happy Birthday" to me while trying to not roll their eyes, much less an entire room of friends. I'd never had a surprise party thrown for me, either, because Chris isn't the surprise type of guy. I know every present I'm getting weeks in advance, and not just because we share the same Amazon account and he hides my gifts in places like the Pringles shelf of the pantry. It felt a little indulgent to spend money and resources on myself, but every time I had that thought, I'd push it away and channel Sally O'Malley from *SNL*. "I'M FIFTY. FIFTY YEARS OLD," I'd think, and hitch up my pants. Sometimes I'd even kick and punch if nobody was around to watch.

Molly Shannon's brilliant Sally O'Malley character was actually the inspiration for my party because one year, on a family trip to New Orleans, we were in a famous restaurant called Mama's, and I looked up from my gumbo to see a parade of ten women all dressed in giant Sally wigs and red stretch suits stagger into the place. They were drunk, wild, and having the time of their lives celebrating one of the Sallys' fiftieth birthday. I remember staring at them with a mixture of delight and jealousy, wishing I had a group that'd show up for me and do something so weird and fun and borderline arrestable public nuisance. At the time I saw them, I didn't have those kinds of friends. But by the time I turned fifty, I did.

It was time for the famous Wendi Fifti Parti of November 2017. I'm sorry you weren't invited. You would have loved it.

The name "Wendi Fifti Parti" was the brainchild of my friend Lauren, an incredibly creative person who does everything well except correctly estimate merchandise quantities. That's why my attic is currently filled with two-hundred Wendi Fifti Parti t-shirts and five-hundred Wendi Fifti Parti cups. (Let me know if you'd like me to send you any. Only five dollars plus flat rate shipping.) Lauren was instrumental in planning the Wendi Fifti Parti at my friend Liz's in-law's gorgeous lakefront home on Lake Buchanan, about twenty miles outside of Austin. (Again, by this age, if at all possible, you should know at least a few people who own lakefront homes.) Unlike my fortieth birthday in Santa Fe, when the group did touristy things, all I wanted to do this time around was stay in the house and shoot the shit. No activities, no group massages, no fancy dinners, no "Excuse me, ma'am, did someone call the Hot Cops?" stripper-grams. I wanted quality facetime with my people who I don't see in person very often.

In the ten years since my last milestone birthday, I'd attained a completely new group of friends. People say you don't make new friends after a certain age, but that's 100 percent bullshit. In fact, let's talk about finding friends as a middle-aged adult for a minute, and then I'll get back to the parti.

Once your kids get older, the Bunco and MLM party invitations dry up, which was understandable in my case considering I usually yelled, "PYRAMID SCHEME, NO THANK YOU!" whenever anyone mentioned the suburban scourges LuLaRoe or Rodan + Fields. I had friends all over the country, but it was important to me to also have locals who I could call on a moment's notice and say, "Hey, want to go to the movies to hate-watch the new Kate Hudson rom-com with me today?" or "Up for lunch?" or "I'm not okay, can you go for a walk?"

And here's how I found them.

But first, remember those Bus Stop Bitches that wouldn't talk to me because they "had enough friends"? (Brief pause while I scowl and mutter a string of swear words.) Unlike them, I've never, ever thought that way. For fuck's sake, there's no limit to how many friends you can have. Or should have. Or will ever have. There are levels of closeness, sure, but the universe doesn't have a THAT'S ENOUGH FOR YOU, DUMMY alarm that'll blare whenever you ask a new person out to coffee.

There's also no age limit to when you can make a friend. Maybe you met your best friend in grade school, and if so, that's wonderful for you. But maybe you won't meet your best friend until you're in your seventies and sitting in the back of a library meeting and someone mentions the book *Twilight* and the woman next to you whispers, "Shirtless teenage vampires can suck it," and then you whisper back, "That's a joke that works on two levels," and boom—you have your bestie for the next twenty years. It's silly to think that you can age out of befriending a new person, especially when we continue to grow and evolve and maybe even find ourselves living a whole new life due to divorce or relocation or something else entirely. That's when you need friends the most.

Here's my simple tip: give and receive. I mean that in the connection sense. I can't even remember how many times I've said to someone, "You have to meet my friend X. You two have so much in common." Or someone has said to me, "You must meet my friend X. You have the same sense of humor." It's basically just friend matchmaking, and to me, it's invaluable. Be generous with your own introductions and know that when anyone else gives you the opportunity to meet one of their friends, it's a gift.

A few years ago, my good friend Meredith had a birthday dinner in downtown Austin. There were about ten of us there, and someone

I'M WEARING TUNICS NOW

suggested we go around the table and say how we each knew Meredith. My answer was "a woman named Trish introduced us years ago," which was true even though we've both since lost touch with Trish. But by far the most popular answer that night? "I met Meredith through Wendi." I didn't realize it until that moment, but it was true. I *had* introduced most of them to Meredith and to each other.

I didn't plan it or strategize it or even realize I was doing it, but it seems that in the past ten years I've become what my friends Lauren and Liz jokingly call "a super connector." They also sometimes call me "Aggressive Networker Aarons" if we're at an event and I say something like, "Have you two met Susan? She also likes eating cheese!" before I run away to fix my Spanx. But if I like this person and I like that person, why not introduce them to each other so we can all like each other and then go out for margaritas together? Why not form a little coven? It's never a bad idea to widen your circle, so look for opportunities to do so.

Sometimes the matchmaking doesn't work, of course, and that's okay. I've definitely gone to lunch with women I didn't click with, and vice versa. I've also gotten along with someone online, and then realized I didn't like them as much offline when we finally met in person, and vice versa. Once I had coffee with a woman who told me five minutes into it, "Huh, you're a lot more boring in person than you are when I read your *Us Weekly* Fashion Police captions." I smiled and answered, "Do you want me to start making fun of your outfit?"

So here's my advice: Be open. Be interested. Be interest*ing*. If you read an article in the newspaper that you like, find the author's email and send them a quick note. That's how I met my friend Stephani. If you see someone post about going to a political rally you support, send them a DM and ask if you can meet them there. That's how I met my friend Jennifer. If you're at an event and someone walks in alone and looks overwhelmed, wave them over to your table and say something cheesy like, "Saved you a seat!" That's how I met my friend Penny—when she saved me a seat. You never age out of the lunchroom credo of "Be nice to the new kid."

By midlife, you know who you are and you know what a friendship means, both good and bad. You know that life is hard. That's why we all need connection and community and love and support, and it doesn't always come from our family. We all want to giggle on the phone late at night with a friend about the stupid *Sex and the City* remake that we can't stop watching or cry to a friend about our kids leaving the nest for college. We all want to be one of the *Golden Girls*. Middle age is not only one of the best times in your life to make new friends, it's also when you need them the most. Okay, friendship lesson over.

Back to the parti.

My guests included Mariana and Isabel, who flew in from New York City, Melisa from Knoxville, Vikki from Minneapolis, Laurie from the Baltimore area, Ann from Madison, Nancy from Oakland, Lisa from Pasadena, and Liz, Lauren, Elizabeth, Stacy, Anne, MJ, Jenny, and Laura from Austin. I'm still amazed and honored that they all spent the time and money to join me on my birthday, and it was by far one of the most fun weekends I've ever had. The cherry on the sundae? Right after they all got into town, we went to lunch at a local TexMex restaurant, and while I was sitting there in the booth, smack in the middle of my fun and loud and interesting friends, I looked up. And there, staring at me with a giant scowl, was the mean chocolate fountain mom I'd heard gossiping about me in the hallway all those years ago.

I immediately tuned out my friends, looked at her with a grin, and then I threw my arms in the air and yelled, "HOW YA LIKE ME NOW, ASSHOLE? GET A LOAD OF DESE APPLES!"

Okay, I only did that in my head, and I think I also just got the *Good Will Hunting* quote wrong, but it was good enough that she saw me with a table of friends. And also that she tripped and spilled a bit of her soda when she was leaving.

I had no doubts that the Wendi Fifti Parti would be weird and wonderful, but it was confirmed the second I walked into the lake house and saw everyone wearing tiny glitter top hats (tiny hats: one of my well-known phobias) and dancing next to a six-foot standee of Barry Manilow that they'd draped in leis and a leather jacket. "It's Barry!" Melisa yelled. "He's here for your party! Looks like you've made it, lady!" (Real friends accept and appreciate that you're a Fanilow, even if they don't quite understand it. That said, I've now convinced five of the people at that party to go to a Manilow show with me.) (And I must note that Melisa is a *long-time* Fanilow otherwise she will send me endless angry texts after she reads this.)

The weekend was perfect and easy and fun, with no fights or squabbles or hair-pulling and wrestling on the floor. The only injuries we incurred were sore stomachs from too much laughing and too much queso. We didn't have any "Are you sleeping with my husband?" drama because nobody was sleeping with anyone else's husband. Mostly because we're all way too tired to take on another responsibility at this point and also, yuck. Who does that? My group of women all know and love each other, and we're over the petty shit that could consume us when we were younger. The weekend's unsaid rules were things like, if you drink, have a margarita. If you don't, there's coffee. If you want to go to sleep early, whatever. If you want to stay up until 3 a.m., that's fine too. Wear jeans and t-shirts or sweatpants or whatever you want, nobody cares. And if you want to commandeer the karaoke mic and sing boy band hits for two straight hours complete with choreographed drill team moves, nobody will stop you, Stacy and Liz. We'll make fun of you and take blackmail video to be used at a later date, but you knew that going in, didn't you? Perhaps the only lowlight of the weekend was the moment they all wore Wendi Fifti Parti shirts and held printed cardboard photo versions of my face on sticks and did a group dance to "Copacabana." You'd think I'd enjoy that, but no. It's now permanently in my brain's "Recurring Nightmare" lobe. It was like something from a low-budget Swedish horror movie where everyone dies a gruesome death except me and Lola the Showgirl.

Another highlight of the weekend were my birthday presents, which I was happy to see weren't thoughtful things like jewelry, charity donations, or gift cards to Chico's because that's where people think fifty-year-olds shop for motherfucking tunics. No, the Fifti Parti gifts were instead *objets d'art* like Lisa's commissioned framed drawing of me and young Barry Manilow; a scrapbook made by my friend Melisa that included letters from my crush, the mayor of Austin, plus notes from Sonya Morgan of *The Real Housewives of New York City* and Maria Bamford, one of my favorite comics. There was also an original Typewriter Rodeo poem from my friend Liz and a one-armed pink boob pillow given to me by my friend Jenny for reasons only she and her collection of taxidermized animals understands. The pillow is now happily sitting in my office chair where it regularly startles visitors.

It was all fun and easy and a good time, but we could have done anything and I would have been happy because I was with the people I was meant to find. It just took me a little longer than expected.

Here's what that last milestone birthday taught me: Eat the cake. Throw the party. Sing and dance, then sing and dance some more, even if you're terrible at it and you probably are because there's only one Beyoncé. Buy the stupid black streamers. And the fake gravestones. And the other party decorations that signify you're almost dead. Laugh at the "Lordy, Lordy, Look Who's 40" cards and your new AARP membership card (but save it for the discounts). Hell, wrestle your rival on the winery floor if the opportunity presents itself and you think you can take her. I don't want to sound like an Instagram inspirational meme, and I know I'm getting close to that vibe, but I 100 percent believe that the best way to handle a big birthday is to embrace it like it's a puppy carrying a plate of warm cookies. Latch onto it like it's naked Daniel Craig. When my friend Meredith was a bit melancholy about turning fifty last year, I insisted that she start making plans. "Get something, anything, on the calendar," I said so she'd spend more time anticipating that than she would dwelling on the looming number that ends in zero. She took my advice, and now her fiftieth birthday memory is of a big, fun dinner in New Orleans with friends and family, and not of a night home alone crying in a bathtub and listening to Adele on Spotify. That's right, I'm pretty much a lifestyle guru now.

On the last night of my crazi funni silli Fifti Parti weekend, my group of friends presented me with probably the weirdest and most wonderful thing anyone has ever done in my honor: they performed a live reading of an episode of *The Facts of Life*. I still don't know why that show was chosen, or that episode, or why they fought over who got to be Natalie and not Jo, who in my opinion was the true breakout star of that show and not just because she always seemed like she wanted to choke Blair, but watching my caring, no bullshit, ride-or-die friends perform a dramatic reading of a bad '80s family sitcom while we relaxed in a beautiful lake house was something I'll never forget. Midway through the weekend, I spent a moment in bittersweet reflection that it took me this long—fifty years—to find these friends and this confidence. I wish I'd known at age thirty how much I'd like myself in twenty years. Man, do I wish that. I even tried to share that sentiment with the group, but since I was tipsy at the time, all they heard was, "Siddhi eviepsy a yayyyy!" and then the *NSYNC singing started up again.

As for documenting that birthday blowout on social media? Posting picture after picture showing off our wild midlife woman weekend on Instagram and Facebook, complete with a dedicated hashtag? Starting up a bit of FOMO online? We were having too much of a good time to remember to do it.

FIFTY CANDLES

Samantha "Sam" Baker wakes up on her fiftieth birthday. She reaches for the iPhone on the nightstand and immediately feels a tear in her rotator cuff. She heads into the bathroom to pluck the white chin hair that grew overnight.

Sam enters the kitchen, anticipating a special breakfast with her family. Instead, she finds her husband watching the latest Trump news on CNN and her teenage daughter posing for a selfie while licking a can of Rockstar Energy Drink. "Oh, hi," her husband finally says. "If you're looking for the Pepcid AC, I took the last one. This fucking guy, am I right?"

Next, Sam goes to her Barre Method class and pays twenty-five dollars to squeeze her glutes next to her best friend Randy. During class, Sam texts Randy that she would definitely do it with Jake Ryan if she had the chance. "Jake Ryan, the divorced dad who was convicted of embezzling from the youth soccer league?" Randy texts back. She includes three eggplant emojis.

"No, I'd do it with Jake Ryan, the divorced dad who was busted for holding illegal poker games in his apartment complex," Sam replies. "But he doesn't even know I exist. Hey, do you have any Icy Hot in your Kate Spade crossbody? My left hamstring is seizing."

What Sam doesn't know is that she accidentally sent the text to Jake Ryan, whose number she has in her phone from that time they worked the dunk tank together at the school carnival.

While waiting in line at Starbucks, Jake gets the text and realizes Sam has the hots for him. Then he goes back to looking at twenty-five-year-old massage therapists named Kayleigh on Tinder.

Later, Sam takes an Uber home after day drinking at a wine bar. The driver is a guy known as Farmer Ted because he grows medical marijuana and heirloom tomatoes under his deck. He asks her to go with him to a protest march later that night and she replies, "Gah! Is Trump all anyone can think about?"

At home, Sam sees she's been kicked out of her bedroom because her husband rented it on Airbnb to a couple from Seattle who make bespoke wedding tuxes for pugs. Not only did her entire family miss her birthday, but now she has to sleep on the Crate & Barrel sectional she spent weeks deciding on with her decorator?

"I can't believe it. They fucking forgot my birthday," Sam sighs. Then she looks through the mail and realizes that the AARP sure didn't.

The Seattle hipsters brought with them a foreign student named Long Duk Dong. Sam takes him to the anti-Trump march later that night and tells him, "I hope nobody yankies your wanky!" Later, Long Duk tweets from his @TheDonger account, "TFW your honky host is straight-up racist."

At the march, Sam ogles Jake who's waving a sign that says TINY HANDS HUGE ASSHOLE with his hot millennial hookup, Karolina. Karolina is totally rocking her pink pussy hat, which makes Sam sad because it's impossible for perimenopausal women to wear headgear without sweating to death.

Upset, Sam leaves the protest to cry in her Volvo. Farmer Ted finds her and captures it on Facebook Live. Then he asks for her Spanx to sell on eBay, and she obliges. "I can't believe I gave my Spanx to a geek," she groans. "Now my FUPA will be totally visible through my Lululemon."

Jake leaves the march with Karolina, who's throwing a pop-up hang at Jake's ex-wife's house while she's out of town on a yoga retreat. After Jake becomes furious that Karolina's friends don't appreciate the "80s on 8" channel on Sirius XM radio, he sends Sam a DM.

Unfortunately, she doesn't get it because her phone ran out of battery while she was tracking her teenage daughter's trip to the frozen yogurt shop.

Hours later, Jake tries to make a deal with Farmer Ted: Sam's Spanx in exchange for Jake's hookup Karolina, who is blackout drunk. Farmer Ted says, "Seriously, bro? Have you ever heard of a little thing called CONSENT? JFC, it's not 1986, you caveman," and he drives Karolina to her mother's house and doesn't even charge her the Uber surge rate.

The next day is Sam's daughter's TEDx Talk about the struggle of white girl feminism, but she has her period and she's also drugged up on whatever was in the vape sesh she just did with her friends, so the TEDx Talk is a disaster. After a moment of reflection, Sam's family finally realizes they forgot her fiftieth birthday because they've been so distracted by the problems of Trump and social media. Sam doesn't accept their apology, however, and says, "Whatever, losers. I bought my own present, and it's a trip to Paris by myself. Good luck trying to figure out how the dishwasher works."

She bravely walks out of the TEDx Talk only to see Jake Ryan waiting for her in the Porsche he leased after the divorce and now totally regrets because of the gas mileage and also, he looks like a d-bag in it. He drives her to his apartment and presents her with a gluten- and dairy-free birthday cake that is aflame with fifty candles. The moment before they throw it in the sink so the fifty candles don't catch the curtains on fire, Jake smiles and tells Sam to make a wish.

Sam replies, "I'm fifty years old, motherfucker. I don't have time for wishes." Jake leans in for a kiss, but she's already on her way out the door to the airport.

CHAPTER SIXTEEN

I'M WEARING BADASS NOW

It's a bright, sunny Saturday afternoon in January of 2020, and I'm standing on the steps of the Texas Capitol. It's the same building I'd walked into years earlier to witness Wendy Davis's filibuster, but this time things are different. For starters, there's a podium in front of me, and I'm about to make a speech. I look out at the huge crowd of young and old women, some men, and a few toddlers, all holding signs and chanting and cheering. Like me, they're here to fight to make the world better because it's been a rough few years on all of us. Sitting behind me are my friends Meredith and Kathy, who will also be speaking, and my friend Shellie, the organizer of this Austin Women's March. I'm ready to start talking about getting out the vote and women's rights and abortion rights and equality, but before the first word comes out of my mouth, I pause to let the moment sink in. I think of how far I'd come, from a lost stay-at-home mom looking for her place in life, to here, invited to use my voice because people want to hear it. The day feels hopeful. It feels like a fresh start for all of us.

Six weeks later, we'd all be trapped in our homes with sourdough starter, no toilet paper, and *Tiger King*.

The momentum and plans I had that January day, that everyone had, came to a crashing halt in early 2020 due to the COVID-19 pandemic that, as of this writing, is still going strong. Maybe by the time you read this, things will be better and people won't be punching flight attendants over wearing masks on airplanes. I sure hope so and not just because that led to Southwest Airlines ending the in-flight booze service that I've relied on for years. I'm incredibly grateful for scientists and doctors and frontline workers, and for the vaccines that I love enough to be jabbed every day if I were allowed. (#TeamPfizer) But it's been a tough time.

My family was more fortunate than many during quarantine, with no lost loved ones or jobs or much hardship besides most of our plans and activities being put on hold. Sam, my first baby, the one I lugged to Gymboree classes when I was serial killer mom and the one I missed like crazy when he started kindergarten, graduated high school in 2020. It was a little anticlimactic considering it was a slide show on the computer, but at least we didn't have to pay for a cap and gown. He unfortunately had to spend all of his freshman year of college at home, which was nice for me, but it felt like he had one foot out the door the whole time. I know that's a good thing, even if it doesn't always feel that way. It's what we as parents work toward from the time we leave them crying with a babysitter we're not quite sure we trust. I still remember that October day in 2001 when Chris and I brought newborn Sam home from the hospital. We stood in the nursery and looked at each other in wonder and said, "They're . . . just letting us take a baby?"

Now it's, "They're . . . just letting the baby leave home?"

Note: I may have to take a break when writing this chapter to either sob or slug back a cocktail or both, so feel free to join me in the crying closet. It's nice and dark in there!

I thought I was prepared for this time of life, and I've definitely made efforts to find purpose and work and friends, but it still stings. I suppose the only way to ensure that your emotional middle age/ menopause years don't coincide with your emotional empty nest years is to have babies when you're still in high school. That wasn't an option for me because the only dates I had in high school were the due dates on my library books, so here I am now, graying, wrinkled, and on the verge of wandering around Target smiling creepily at babies when Jack graduates in a few months and heads off to his future too. I know I'm making it sound like they're both maverick astronauts flying to Mars or something when all they're doing is going to college, but it feels like the end of an era. It feels like the family dynamic we had for eighteen years will never again be the same. I know it won't.

Seriously, come join me here in the closet. I found a sleeve of Thin Mints in my sock drawer.

Chris and I will be more than okay as we move on to what comes next in our AARP life. Cruises? Elks Lodges? Archeological digs? All of the other activities you see sprightly seniors do in pharmaceutical ads? I know this because we've gone through transitions and hard times before. We've moved, and lost jobs, and gained jobs, and had sick babies, and had years when we panicked about the tax bill and other years when it felt like everything in the house decided to break at the same time. We're too tired to really grapple with any marriage power struggles anymore and too old to care about shit like who left a plate in the sink. Mostly, we're lucky that we still like each other a lot, and love each other more. (Except for whenever he chews.)

The pandemic gave us all time to stay home and sit and reflect on life, and that's exactly what I did. I thought a lot about how bittersweet it is to know there's more road behind you than ahead of you in middle age. I guess fifty isn't even middle age unless you live to one hundred. (Which I might because I take a daily gummy multivitamin from Target.) It was hard to resist the temptation of ruminating on what I should have done or could have done. To not regret mistakes made. To not look at old pictures and wish I still had that body or that hair or that elastic skin. Still, in my heart of hearts, I know I don't want to go back and be that confused, unconfident thirty-year-old crying on her birthday. I don't want to be the insecure mom not saying what she really thinks. I don't want to be interviewing for jobs that I don't like or wearing clothes that don't fit or spending time with people who make me feel bad for no real reason other than they're just not my people. I don't want to go back and be any of the past versions of myself.

I want to be who I am now.

On that day in Austin, the crowd waited for me to start my speech, but I took a second to look at my phone first. I saw texts from Sam and Jack that said, "Good luck, mom!" and "I'm proud of you! love you!" and one from Chris that said, "Can you bring home milk?" quickly followed by another one that said, "You are going to be GREAT!" with a bunch of heart emojis. I felt nervous but I also felt weirdly confident. My knees didn't even shake that much. I knew I might screw up and that I'd maybe (probably) offend someone, but that was okay. I'd reached the age where I have wisdom to share, and if someone doesn't like it, I don't really care. I'm fresh out of fucks.

I admit that a small part of me wished my jeans weren't so snug around my menopot belly, wished I didn't need to wear trifocal glasses to read the speech in my hand, and really wished everyone who took my photo would remember to put a great wrinkle-erasing filter on it. But that was it, and I know those wishes are stupid. That day and every day since, I remind myself to be happy to be this age and this person and this woman because it's nothing to take lightly. As the sun hit the white marble Goddess of Liberty perched atop the Capitol dome that day, I paused, then I opened my mouth, and yelled, "Good afternoon, Austin! My name is Wendi Aarons, and I know you're going to want to hear what I have to say!"

And then I said it.

CHAPTER SEVENTEEN

I'M WEARING TUNICS NOW

You've probably all noticed that I recently switched up my personal style. That's right, I'm wearing tunics now. That's what this gorgeous piece of fabric draping my body is called. A tunic. It originates at my shoulders, meanders down my chest and stomach like a cool, mountain stream, and ends its magnificent journey by lightly caressing my hips like a lover who's just kind of phoning it in these days. It is my tunic. And it is perfection.

The word "tunic" most likely means something in another language, like Greek or Latin, but who gives a shit because in English, "tunic" means "suddenly, shopping at Chico's doesn't seem so gross anymore." Because much like death, Jesus, or one of those square buzzy things they use at the Chili's hostess stand, the tunic knows when your time has come. And baby, your time will come.

The tunic comes for all.

One day my middle-aged pudge was happily crammed into my usual tight Old Navy tank top that says GIMME CATS AND LATTES, then boom. The very next day an invisible hand grabbed me by the neck and pushed me into my mom's section of Macy's. There I wandered dreamlike until I found the Holy Grail. The motherlode. The rack of Stretch Organic Cotton Jersey Tunics waiting for me under the fluorescent lights and warm bath of the piped-in Muzak. These tunics weren't marked down, not even by a paltry 20 percent, but

I didn't care. I didn't care one fucking bit. I hastily yanked my Visa out of my purse and gasped, "Put it on my card! Put them all on my card! No matter the predatory interest rate!" Friends, I'm not embarrassed to admit that I paid full retail for those damn Stretch Organic Cotton Jersey Tunics. I had no choice. There was no resisting it. Because much like Eileen Fisher's corporate messaging would say if I worked at Eileen Fisher and they let me write their corporate messaging, one doesn't simply wear a tunic. When you're a woman over forty, a tunic wears you.

Now that I'm wearing tunics, I've thrown away the regular shirts that have suppressed me my entire life. Regular shirts are straightjackets. Corsets. Regular shirts conceal nothing. Torso, upper arms, hips, all of that bullshit is displayed in a regular shirt, like slabs of ham in a deli case. But in my tunic? In my tunic you can't see any of the middle part of my middle-aged body. I'm shrouded in mystery. I'm a stylish enigma. I'm a graying fortune cookie with a fortune inside it that says, "Fuck you, I was in shape in the '80s."

In my tunic, I'm The Man Behind the Curtain. No, The Woman Inside the Curtain. And nobody knows what's going on inside the curtain. It hides every secret. Did I just do two-thousand sit-ups or did I just eat an entire Boston cream pie that I found in the back of the freezer? Is my lower back bare or is it inked in a regrettable tramp stamp that says "American Skank" in Chinese characters? Am I an apple bottom or a kumquat bottom? Is my stomach untouched or is it covered in leeches because of some stupid holistic thing I'm testing out for my idiot brother-in-law Gary's new "wellness center"? Nobody knows. Nobody cares. Nobody can even imagine. Why? Because I'm wearing motherfucking tunics now.

Sometimes when I'm feeling subdued, which is the fancy way I say, "hungover from draining a box of pinot grigio," I switch out my tunic for a tunic-adjacent item: the long, lightweight sweater. Long, lightweight sweaters are magic, and they come in a wide spectrum of colors ranging from light beige to medium beige to dark beige. And per store policy, they are only sold to women born before 1980. Sorry, it's true. Don't even try to lie because they'll check your ID, youngblood. Long, lightweight sweaters are soft, they are silent, and they are the length of a fairly tall twelve-year-old boy named Jeremy. "What does wearing a long, lightweight sweater feel like" you ask? Why, I'll tell you what it feels like: it feels like being inside one of those caterpillar cocoons your kids had in their elementary classroom, except with less oozing and more cashmere. It feels like being back inside the womb.

Whenever I'm out and about in my long, lightweight sweater, strangers ask me if I'm a therapist. "Can you help me?" they ask. "Can you solve my problems? Can you keep me off the ledge, ma'am?" I gaze at them with a Mona Lisa smile, then I put my hands in the Namaste position, and whisper, "I am not a therapist. I only look like one. Any advice I give you would most definitely make your mental health rapidly decline. But if you buy me a nonfat latte, I will find motivational quotes on Instagram and read them to you in a soothing voice."

Back to tunics.

When I'm in my tunic, I'm ready for anything that's expected of a woman over forty. If a Nancy Meyers movie needs an extra for a beach house brunch scene, give me a call. If someone is needed to stand in front of a crowd and stare commandingly until they quiet the hell down, I'm ready to go. What's that? The Active Adult Senior Living center needs a more-cute-than-pretty, affordable model for their new ad campaign? Hand me a can of Ensure and a tennis racket and tell me to smile, bucko. I'm ready for my close-up. Put my mug on those junk mail flyers and send them out. Because I am confident, I am fashionable, and I am ensconced in three-to-five yards of kicky magenta linen.

How old am I? I'm tunic years old.

Remember, friends, a tunic is not a caftan. A tunic is not a toga. A tunic isn't one of those stupid muumuus sold at flea markets for a dollar. A tunic is never in style or out of style; a tunic transcends style. But most of all, a tunic is a woman's way of saying, "You know what? Nobody's looking at me anymore anyway, so why not just relax and throw out my fucking shapewear? Why not be comfortable and self-assured for once in my goddamn life?" Yeah, it's pretty much that last one. A glorious, comfortable future awaits.

I'm wearing tunics now.

Acknowledgments

I've literally had years of time to craft this acknowledgments page, but instead I'm writing it two hours before it's due. But I guess that's sort of my life's theme: better late than never.

First, I'd like to thank Brandi Bowles, who I first met when I was working on a book about Sam starting kindergarten and she was a new literary agent. Now Sam is twenty-one and Brandi is a hugely successful literary agent. Her enthusiasm and support 100 percent made this happen. Second, thank you to my wonderful editor, Allison Adler, at Andrews McMeel Publishing for appreciating, championing, and shaping my midlife voice into something even better than it was.

So many friends are part of this journey (yes, I just said "journey" and I'm not even on *The Bachelor*), and I'm thankful for early readers—Janelle Hanchett, Ann Imig, Nancy Davis Kho, Mariana Olenko, and Melisa Wells; plus my Austin early readers and cheer squad—Kathy Valentine, Meredith Walker, and Anne Hebert. Thanks also go to KJ Dell'Antonia, Jessica Lahey, Cassie Jones Morgan, Gloria Fallon, Marilyn Naron, and Devorah Blachor. I couldn't get through my days (or nights) without my Tiny Texter crew that includes Lisa Rosenberg, Elizabeth McGuire, Vikki Reich, Lauren Bayne, and Laurie White. And a big shout-out to my Bee Cave crew—Stacy Libby, Amanda Beth Hill, and Elizabeth Hight—and my most loyal and enthusiastic supporter, Sandra Rabbin, who recently sent me THC gummies in a sock (which totally didn't happen if you're reading this and work for the FBI).

When I was a lonely stay-at-home mom, McSweeney's Internet Tendency proved to be a lifeline so thank you to everyone involved from 2009 up until now, including the great Chris Monks. Thanks also to Emily Flake, proprietress of St. Nell's Humor Writing Residency, where I wrote a lot of this book. Okay, I just wrote one chapter and drank a lot of wine, but it's a process. To the OG bloggers, and the *Listen to Your Mother* people, and my humor writing peers, and to anyone that's ever read my work online, and laughed, or liked it, or shared it, thank you. It's the best feeling in the world to connect with someone because of something you wrote.

My incredible parents, Sharon and Wayne Willson, have supported and encouraged my writing for my entire life, and I'm so damn lucky to have them. I can't wait to celebrate this book at the Elk's Club with them and with my lovely sisters, Lisa Lucas and Amy Delaney. All of us in tunics, of course.

Finally, to my sons, Sam and Jack—being your mother is a million times better than I ever could have imagined. I'm so proud of you both, even if you just pretended to read the entire book and then skipped to this page. And to Chris, the man I met over a keg in Reno when I was a dumb twenty-one-year-old, and who's stuck with me all these years through all of our ups and downs and sideways, and who says things like, "Shouldn't you be writing?" I love you.

About the Author

Wendi Aarons is a writer and humorist whose work has frequently appeared in outlets like McSweeney's and *The New Yorker*, among many others. She and her tunics live in Austin.